Greek Mythology

An Enthralling Overview of Greek Myths,
Gods, and Goddesses

Free limited time bonus

Stop for a moment. We have a free bonus set up for you. The problem is this: we forget 90% of everything that we read after 7 days. Crazy fact, right? Here's the solution: we've created a printable, 1-page pdf summary for this book that you're reading now. All you have to do to get your free pdf summary is to go to the following website: **https://livetolearn.lpages.co/enthrallinghistory/** Once you do, it will be intuitive. Enjoy, and thank you!

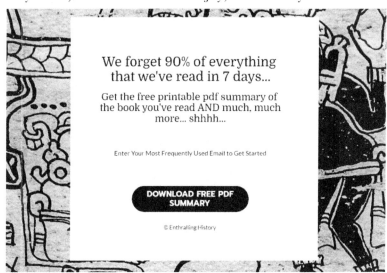

We forget 90% of everything that we've read in 7 days...

Get the free printable pdf summary of the book you've read AND much, much more... shhhh...

Enter Your Most Frequently Used Email to Get Started

DOWNLOAD FREE PDF SUMMARY

© Enthralling History

Contents

Introduction

Similar to other kinds of mythologies within a pagan-based society, Greek mythology has adjusted itself throughout the centuries. It has been at the whims of redactors, philosophers, and storytellers who shifted narratives for the purposes of revealing some deeper meaning about the actions of gods, goddesses, and heroes.

For instance, the birth of the god of wine, Dionysus, is hotly debated and has been rewritten multiple times. In the version composed by Hesiod, Dionysus was born of Zeus and Semele, a princess. In another version composed by Hesychius, he is the son of Dione, a female Titan. The switch in mothers is by no means a coincidence; the two men could have heard the story differently, or they could have made the adjustments themselves.

This diversity reflects the variation of realities in the Greek world. Greece was not considered to be a united kingdom in the sense that there was one monarch who ruled over all of Greece. The mainland and islands were governed under distinct *poleis* (singular *polis*, meaning "city"), which led to great variations in Greek culture, art, literature, and oral histories. The diversity of that world is reflected in this book, which seeks to marry the different versions of myths together in an attempt to represent the whole of the Greek world and the surrounding nations.

Our main goal is to bestow a comprehensive and compelling worldview of Greek mythology in all the multifaceted aspects that go into good storytelling. The versions of these myths below are very much in the spirit of mythology. They might be a bit different than the myths you remember at times, as we have sometimes taken the more dramatic version of a myth and married it into its traditional telling, but the core of the story will remain the same.

Chapter One – From Chaos to Uranus

Which came first, the chicken or the egg? The creation of the world for many ancient cultures, including the Greeks, began with a place where there was no beginning and no end. It began in Chaos, a deep but not entirely empty void. Chaos would give birth to the first gods. The primordial ones' hot-headed and ballsy (pay attention because there is a great joke there) behavior gave birth to a world that would soon be engulfed in the drama of their children.

It is unclear whether Chaos's children gave birth to themselves, springing forth from the emptiness of their sire, or if Chaos squatted low and painfully birthed these beings. Also highly debated amongst scholars is the gender of Chaos, who, for the sake of argument, we shall consider to be female. This makes sense since she delivered a couple of kids, but the gender and biology of the Greek gods, Titans, and other miscellaneous non-human characters are not dictated by the black and white laws of biology. In Greek mythology, babies could be born from a head, a thigh, a volcano under the earth, or a dark swirling black hole at the beginning of time.

And so, Chaos gave birth to Gaia, whose body would lay the foundations for the earth, which would spring all forms of life. The second born was Tartarus, who is also referred to as Erebus. His body comprised the underworld, the realm of the dead, where all souls went for judgment at the end of their life. Both gods and men feared what lay in the darkness of the underworld. After Tartarus came Pontus, who was the first god of the sea. But he was more than this—he was the sea itself, a raw form of power that would be inherited by the godly generations that came later. This was the case with all the primordial beings. They were the stadium in which the Olympians played their games, and they were also the source of the Olympians' weapons and power.

Chaos also gave birth to other children considered to be among the original primordial beings. Eros, the fabled and cherub-like god of love, who some consider to be the child of the Olympians Aphrodite and Ares, is actually believed to have been born at the beginning of time. Nyx, the literal night who took the form of a woman, also emerged from Chaos. Her name and characterization as a shadowy figure can give you the impression that she is evil. However, she is an ambivalent goddess, holding both light and dark qualities, which would be embodied by her numerous children.

Nyx and her brother Erebus brought Aether and Hemera into the world. Aether filled up the space between the heavens and the earth with a fine mist that gave the sky its blue hue. His sister-wife Hemera, the literal day, was an entirely independent entity from Helios (the sun), and she brought forth her brother's mists each morning. Oftentimes, the sibling-partner combinations in Greek mythology represent the duality of the natural world, such as the water and the rain cycle.

Nyx also gave birth to several other divine beings, pushing them out from her own dark mass. These children shaped a vast range of human experiences, both positive and negative. This list is lengthy, but there was Moros (fate), Hypnos (sleep), Oneiroi (dreams),

Geras (old age), Oizys (pain), Nemesis (revenge), Eris (strife), Apate (deceit), Philotes (sexual pleasure), Momos (blame), Thanatos (peaceful death), Ker (violent death), and finally the Hesperides (the daughters of the evening who were typically depicted as nymphs). During this same time, Nyx's sister Gaia birthed her son Uranus, who would become the lord of the entire cosmos. Their union would produce the old gods of Greece, the famed and ferocious Titans.

Chapter Two – The Titans

It is safe to say that out of all the divine beings of Greek mythology, Gaia and Uranus were overachievers when it came to the number of children. Not only did they produce hundreds of children, but they also gave birth to several different types of monsters and Titans. Uranus was determined to have not only as many children as possible but also perfect children with considerable gifts and beauty. Their firstborn children were not a success, at least according to Uranus. These were the three Hecatonchires. These accursed monsters, with their hundred hands and fifty heads to one body, were the least favored amongst Uranus and Gaia's children.

Their second attempt at children resulted in three one-eyed Cyclopes. These children were closer to what their father had hoped for, as they were born with unmatched physical strength and had a prowess for metalworking. Later, the Cyclopes would form the gods' first weapons.

Still, Uranus hated his monstrous children. In fact, he hated them so much that he threw them into the deepest and darkest pits of Tartarus. Those children never saw the light of day; instead, they were cast into the darkness as soon as they were pulled from Gaia. This broke her heart. Naturally, she was hesitant to produce any more children for Uranus, but the lord of the heavens gave her little choice in the matter. He would keep going until he had his perfect children. Thankfully, Gaia's next several pregnancies resulted in twelve ideal children, who are known as the Titans.

These twelve beings are referred to in sources as the Uranides. There were six males and six females. Four of the brothers—Coeus, Crius, Hyperion, and Iapetus—held up the heavens and suspended their father Uranus just above the earth. However, the official firstborn was Oceanus, the patron god of fresh water. He was responsible for overseeing the rivers, lakes, aquifers, springs, and even the clouds in the sky. The second-born, Coeus, was the Titan of intellect and questioning. Coeus was also responsible for keeping the northern axis around which the heavens spun, which he held along with three of his brothers.

The next brother, Crius, the Titan and lord of the constellations and the yearly calendar, kept sway over the north axis of the heavens. The next brother, Hyperion, the lord of light, sired the lights that come from the cosmos, including the dawn (Eos), the sun (Helios), and the moon (Selene). The final brother, Iapetus, the Titan of mortality, would give birth to the gods that created humanity.

After the five brothers came their sisters. The female Titans would lay with their brothers and create generations of Titans and gods. Theia was the Titan of foresight and mother to Hyperion's three godly children. Rhea was the goddess of feminine fertility and would soon become the queen of the Titans. Themis, the Titan of the law of fate by which all men must abide, would later become pregnant by her nephew and give birth to the seasons and the Fates, the old crones of time. Next came Mnemosyne, the goddess of memory. She would also give birth to a couple of Muses by the very same nephew that impregnated her sister Themis. The second youngest daughter, Phoebe, the Titan of prophecy, was the wife of "intellect" (her brother Coeus) and the patron goddess of the legendary Oracle of Delphi. The youngest daughter Tethys was the wife of her brother Oceanus and sired for him the source of every freshwater source that would fall under his dominion.

These Titans became the world around which humanity would grow. They were the foundations of knowledge, culture, and tradition. However, there was still one more Titan to be born. Cronos, the youngest, was the Titan of time. And he had all of time's most destructive qualities, such as aging, erosion, and decay. He was by far the most ruthless and hateful of the Titans. He despised his accursed father for the mistreatment of his brothers, the Cyclopes and the Hecatonchires.

Obviously, Gaia was not so thrilled with her husband. She also despised his cruel and greedy nature, as he had forced her to bear him children he either rejected or abused. Over time, her hatred grew deep. It molded itself, forming the first metals of the earth that would be used to fashion a god-killing weapon—the sickle that would destroy Uranus for all time. Gaia approached her children and asked them all to search their hearts and to take up the blade that grew from her hatred and kill Uranus. Her children stood silent, as they were afraid to rise up against the wrath of their father. Cronos, the youngest, was the only one to heed his mother's call. He, along with his brothers who held up the heavens, would concoct a plan to exact terrible vengeance and murder their father.

That night, Uranus returned and brought the darkness of night with him. He laid over his wife, meaning to take her yet again in his lustful greed. Uranus was aroused and prepared to enter Gaia, but before he could, the four pillars of the earth—Coeus, Crius, Hyperion, and Iapetus—seized their father, pinning him down. Cronos leaped forth from the shadows and cut his father from root to stem and tossed his genitals into the sea. The combination of sea and sperm birthed one of the most famous Olympians in history: the goddess of love herself, Aphrodite.

With his dying breath, Uranus spoke his last cruel words to his son Cronos, a terrible prophecy that would lead to the loss of the remainder of Cronos's compassion. He told his son that one day, one of his own children would seek to overthrow him and that they would do to him what he had done to his father.

The Mutilation of Uranus by Saturn (Cronos) *by Giorgio Vasari (1556).*
(Public Domain, https://commons.wikimedia.org/wiki/File:The_Mutilation_of_Uranus_by_Saturn.jpg)

Chapter Three – The War of the Titans

After the fall of Uranus, Cronos usurped his crown as "King of the Cosmos" and took Rhea, his sister, as queen. Despite having succeeded in dispatching their wicked father, the Titans could do nothing to remove the foreboding prophecy from their brother's mind. Uranus had won. Cronos's fear that he would one day be dispatched by his own children turned him into ten times the monster his father was. Upon the birth of each of his children, Cronos swallowed them whole. These were the gods who would take up residence on Mt. Olympus and seize control of the earth and heavens: Hestia, Hera, Demeter, Poseidon, Hades, and Zeus.

The last child, Zeus, was not swallowed but hidden away by his mother Rhea, who gave her husband a rock swaddled in a blanket to consume in Zeus's place. The rest of her children remained alive, continuously growing in their father's stomach. Zeus was raised in secret far away near Mount Ida, which was on the island of Crete. He lived in a cave guarded day and night by the Curetes, and he was nurtured by the milk of Amalthea, a she-goat. When Zeus came to power, he honored Amalthea by placing her likeness in the stars. He fashioned his shield from her hide and created the cornucopia of plenty from her horn. The Curetes were also the children of Gaia, but they were not Titans. They were thought to be the first inhabitants of Crete. They performed the first war dances, banging together their spears and shields so as to drown out the cries of the infant Zeus so that his location would not be discovered.

When Zeus reached manhood, he sought to rise against Cronos, but he needed the help of his siblings. Their father and the Titans were too strong to take on alone. So, Rhea approached her mother Gaia and beseeched her to reveal the secrets of the earth and make her a concoction that would cause Cronos to vomit up his now fully grown children. Metis, the sister of Rhea, presented it to Cronos so that he would not suspect their plan, and he drank the mixture with no hesitation. Up came all of his swallowed children. They, along with their brother Zeus, retreated to the safety of Mt. Olympus and began a terrible ten-year war against Cronos and the Titans. It was the old gods versus the new. Some Titans would be forced to choose sides, and Zeus used all of his wits and strength to recruit the most valuable. Out of the numerous Titans, though, only two would stand against Cronos: Themis, the goddess of divine law and wisdom (daughter of Gaia and Uranus), and her son Prometheus, who would later bestow the gift of knowledge to humanity.

After ten years of war, there seemed to be no victor in sight, and both sides were beginning to lose heart. However, the turning point eventually came, and it was due to the most unlikely allies in the war: the monsters that Uranus had imprisoned in the depths of Tartarus. Cronos, who had vowed to release his brothers from the underworld, had broken his promise and left them to rot away in the dark. Zeus freed his uncles, the Cyclopes and Hecatonchires, from captivity. As a reward, the Cyclopes made Zeus and his brothers weapons of monumental power. They were cast from the forces of nature that stirred inside Gaia and the heavens. These weapons were none other than Zeus's thunderbolt, Poseidon's trident, and Hades's pitchfork.

With the tides now having turned in favor of the Olympians, the last day of the ten-year war, known as the Titanomachy, would occur. This final day of battle, as recorded in Hesiod's *Theogony* (Hesiod was a Greek poet), speaks of the might of the Hecatonchires. With their hundred hands, they hurled down a rain of gargantuan boulders upon the Titans, forcing them to take cover behind the mountains. Zeus delivered the final blow to his father Cronos, and with no more allies or strength to resist his son, the king of the universe and this terrible father of time had been defeated, and he was cast down into the underworld along with his brothers and sisters. Their dark prison would be guarded by its former inhabitants, the hundred-handed Hecatonchires. However, Themis and Prometheus would live since they had aided the gods. Prometheus's brother Atlas, who sided with Cronos, was tasked with holding up the sky as punishment for his crimes.

With their enemies defeated and imprisoned, the Olympians set to the task of deciding who would rule which domains of the earth. The three brothers—Zeus, Poseidon, and Hades—drew lots for the largest kingdoms. Zeus would become the king of the gods, lord of the skies, and the god of thunder and lightning. Poseidon came to rule the vast depths of the sea; he was the shaker of mountains and the creator of new lands. Hades drew the shortest straw, so he was made the lord of the underworld, and he rarely emerged from his dark domain.

Chapter Four – The Gods

Zeus

Zeus was the king of the Gods, the ruler of the heavens and the earth, the manipulator of weather, and the wielder of lightning and thunder. In addition to these many titles, Zeus was also the god of reason and justice. He is shown in representations of Greek wall art and pottery as a man in his later years on account of his well-developed beard and large build. No doubt, the god himself was an attractive and incredibly powerful god, but his greatest strength was his skillful mind. It was through his cunning and prowess that he was able to defeat his numerous enemies and claim the throne of Olympus.

Despite his keen sense of justice and wisdom, Zeus was quite rash in his actions as a god. He was prone to quick decision-making, which probably contributed to the fact that he had more children than most of the other Olympians. Although Zeus technically had several wives, he also had coitus with a number of nymphs and mortal women, producing hundreds of children in the process. Most of these children became notable heroes and figures in Greek mythology, such as Helen of Troy and Perseus, the slayer of the Gorgon Medusa, as well as several major gods and goddesses.

When Zeus first came to power, he took Metis as his wife, the very same Metis who had freed Zeus's siblings from the belly of their father. Metis was the daughter of Oceanus and Tethys, and she was the goddess of good counsel. It is easy to understand Zeus's initial attraction to Metis, and she became his most trusted confidant and mentor. Well, up until the time he swallowed her whole but more on this later.

Zeus had many other wives, both mortal and immortal, but his main queen, at least in keeping with Greek mythological tradition, was his sister Hera. Zeus, like many other gods, could shapeshift, and most of the time, he approached his sexual partners and conquests in the guise of an animal. This was how he won the affections of Hera.

The ancient Greeks connected with the gods through their interactions and usage of the natural world. Zeus was identified with the natural world through symbols like the bull and the eagle or through various species of plant life, mainly the oak tree.

Out of all the qualities a king is meant to possess, perhaps the most important is wisdom. Without a doubt, the kings who last the longest and are the most loved tend to be wise. These are the kings who seek the advice and counsel of others. Zeus took his role as a king very seriously, and he was constantly attended by a multitude of lesser gods, goddesses, and spirits who acted as his advisors and bodyguards. At each foot of his throne sat a guardian spirit: Kratos (Strength), Zelos (Rivalry), Nike (Victory), and Bia (Force). Hermes, one of Zeus's sons, acted as his herald, and the official summons and messages of the king could only be delivered by Iris, the iridescent goddess of the rainbow. After Zeus consumed Metis, the position of the hand of the king was vacant. Themis, the Titan who had stood beside Zeus during the decade-long war with Cronos and the other Titans, was charged with the order and peace of the cosmos and attended the king in all of his endeavors. She even kept her loyalty to Zeus after he banished her son Prometheus to the underworld to undergo the torture of having a vulture (or eagle in some versions) continuously eat his magically regenerating liver until the end of time.

Poseidon

Poseidon, the god of the seas, master of earthquakes, and the creator of new lands and islands, had a temper that was as reckless and destructive as the sea itself. With his great trident, he moved the waters, carrying ships safely across the sea or bringing waves on land and washing away whole villages and cities.

Poseidon was not only destructive. He also possessed a more creative side and manifested the first horses and hippocampi, fish-tailed horses that he used to draw his golden chariot from the sea to Mt. Olympus. His physical appearance is not that different from his brothers. He is often depicted as an older man with a beard, and there is usually a wreath of celery around his head instead of olives like Zeus. One of his natural symbols is the celery stalk; another one is the pine tree.

Just like his brother, Poseidon was tempted by the beauty of mortals, goddesses, and nymphs. However, he was far less of a gentleman than his brother. Calling a spade a spade, Poseidon was a habitual rapist. There are several notable tales of him raping young women, with the two most notable victims being his wife and queen of the seas, the "ebony-eyed" nymph Amphitrite, and his own sister Demeter, whom he took against her will while they were both horses. Rape in the ancient world was not thought of as a crime in the same way it is perceived today. In other ancient sources, including legal corpora, rape was not an act of violence but rather uncontrollable passion. That being said, Poseidon still seemed to have a bit of an issue with the topic more than other gods and goddesses. It was perhaps a way to characterize his wildly violent and rash behavior, as the people could compare his behavior to the sea, an entity that has very little regard for its victims since it cannot control its raging waters.

Poseidon had many affairs with magical beings, including his own grandmother, the primordial being Gaia. Thus, he produced some of the most famous children in Greek mythology. The winged horse Pegasus sprung from the severed head of Poseidon's sexual conquest Medusa. Triton, his son by Amphitrite, controlled and quelled the waves of the Aegean Sea. The depictions of Triton look like something from an Old Spice commercial. Picture a merman with a set of washboard abs and sometimes an unruly beard. Other times, his face was meant to resemble that of a Greek youth, one perhaps around the age of twenty or twenty-five, given the fact that beards signaled a mature age in Greek culture. His symbol is a conch shell. Poseidon's daughter, Rhode, a sea nymph and the goddess protector of the Greek island of Rhodes, would become the wife of Helios, the sun.

Hades

The lord of the underworld was as gloomy as his domain. Hades had a burning resentment toward his siblings for his lot in being looked down upon and rejected as the god of the dead. (He was not the god of death, though; that role belonged to Thanatos.) Although Hades was not prone to common decencies, like manners or smiling, he was the richest of the gods, for all the treasures that lay inside the earth were his property. This is one of the reasons that his most recognizable symbol is the cornucopia, the horn of plenty. At the end of their lives, the dead would be led to the underworld by the wing-footed god Hermes. At the edge of the River Styx, they would wait with two gold coins for the boatman Charon to ferry them across to Hades's dark dominion. The underworld had various sections, and people would be assigned to these sections according to the life they had lived. While the underworld was meant to be a realm for punishment and pain, it was also a place of final rest for those souls deserving of peace.

However, Hades was also the guardian of proper funeral rites, and any soul that did not receive a proper sanctified burial according to the laws of Hades was not allowed to enter the gates of the underworld. This is why Hades kept the gates guarded day and night by his most loyal disciple, the three-headed dog Cerberus. Any sort of dark magic or ritual was the niche of the god of the dead, particularly the cult activity of attempting to raise the dead. If an ancient Greek really wanted their curse on someone to stick, they invoked curses that called upon the powers and prowess of Hades.

Like his brothers, Hades is considered to have the physical appearance of an older man with a dark beard and more of a medium build. Unlike his brothers, however, who seemed to be attracted to just about anyone and everyone, Hades was far more selective with his lovers and often formed deep attachments to them. His main queen was Persephone, the goddess of spring vegetation and the daughter of his own sister Demeter. Although their union deeply upset Persephone's mother, over time, her daughter learned to come to terms with her predicament, and she must have developed at least some sort of feelings for her uncle.

When he went off with his lovers and left her to tend to the underworld alone, she exacted terrible revenge on these women, often throwing her husband into deep grief. One of these women, Minthe, was trampled under the goddess's foot (some versions say Demeter did this). Hades was so distraught that the goddess transformed Minthe's body into a mint plant and named the mountain where she died in her honor. To this day, the site is said to be a very holy domain that the god of the underworld visits often. The other concubine of Hades was Leuce, the daughter of the Titan Oceanus. She was carried off by Hades and also murdered by his wife. However, in later versions, she lived out her days in the underworld. Regardless of the myth you look at, Hades transformed her into a white poplar tree and wears a laurel of poplar leaves around his head as a crown.

The god of the dead was indeed a hopeless romantic, and he showed favor toward heroes that embarked on their quests in the name of love. The singer Orpheus traveled to the underworld to retrieve his recently departed and dearly beloved wife, Eurydice. Hades and Persephone were so moved by his plea that they agreed to release his wife. However, she would trail behind him, and he must not look back, or else she would return to the land of the dead. Orpheus did as he was instructed and did not look back to check for his wife, even though the temptation was great. Right as he stepped foot into the world above, he decided he didn't trust Hades (some say he wanted to make sure she was there, while others say he was so eager that he could wait no longer). He looked back to see if the soul of his wife had indeed followed him out. He turned and saw that it was his wife, and he was filled with unspeakable joy. As a smile crossed his lips, the earth closed its gates, swallowing up Eurydice and taking her back into the darkness.

Hermes

As far as gods go, Hermes is by far the most approachable and likable. This silver-tongued prince was the god of trade, athletics, healthy competition, medicinal knowledge, and thievery. Although this last quality is classically unsavory, Hermes could be considered the original gentleman thief, as he used his finely tuned skills to steal from his marks. Think more along the lines of pickpocketing instead of mugging. Hermes is also rarely ever seen in Greek art without his caduceus, more commonly known as a herald's scepter or that thing you see on the side of ambulances in the United States. At times, he favors his father's looks, sporting a long thick beard, and other times, he is depicted as a young, effeminate, and beautiful man. He is often thought to have the youngest physical appearance of all the Olympians.

Although Hermes was by far the most mischievous and diabolically cunning of all the gods, he was, without a doubt, one of his father's personal favorites. That's saying a lot, considering Zeus had hundreds of children. Hermes started displaying signs of cunning intelligence when he was only an infant. Only a few hours after his birth, he managed to sneak away from his mother Maia as she was resting and stole his brother Apollo's cattle, wiping away their footprints in the dust. Apollo searched high and low for his herd. Little Hermes revealed his cruel actions but would not return the cattle until he was forced to do so.

As a child, Hermes was also a gifted craftsman, and he created the lyre from the shell of a turtle. He gifted this to Apollo in order to appease the sun god over the theft of his cattle. Apollo was so delighted that he relinquished the herd to Hermes willingly and showered him with additional gifts. Zeus was so impressed by this young savant that he gave him a permanent throne on Olympus and made Hermes his personal messenger and attendant of the dead, as he would accompany them to the underworld. With his winged sandals, he traveled fast on the wind, not unlike the comic book hero Flash. Hermes is often equated with any kind of herding activity; whether it's a flock of animals or a flock of souls, Hermes is the god you would call when you want to move a crowd.

The romantic life of the god of messengers was not unlike the other gods on Mt. Olympus. Hermes consorted with mortals and immortals alike. However, unlike his father, who used his shapeshifting to deceive and/or seduce women or his rapist of an uncle Poseidon, Hermes used plenty of sweet words to seduce his lovers. His skills as a smooth talker afforded him the company of some of the most beautiful goddesses and humans of the age, including the goddess of love herself, Aphrodite. The two, in fact, share a son, the love god of intersexuality and androgyny, Hermaphroditus.

Hermes is often considered to be the god of male sexuality, both homosexuality and heterosexuality, making his coupling with the living embodiment of female sexuality logical. Some even say that Hermes took the hero Perseus as a lover. A few of his other notable male lovers were the king of Thebes and a young boy named Crocus, who Hermes mortally wounded in a game of discus. He felt such grief for his actions that he transformed the youth into a beautiful crocus flower.

Apollo

Apollo was the master of the sun. With his great golden chariot, he would bring forth the warmth of Helios each and every morning. He was also the god of medicine, prophecy, healing, and archery. He and his twin sister Artemis were both skilled archers. They could hunt with the skill of most grown mortal men when they were only infants. Apollo was also the patron god of youth, and as such, he is never depicted with a full raging beard like his forefathers.

Apollo's father was Zeus, and his mother was the immortal second-generation Titan Leto, patron goddess of motherhood, modesty, and womanly demure. The story of Apollo's birth, as well as that of his sister Artemis, is similar to other tales that surround the many lovers of Zeus and their offspring. Leto was hunted to the ends of the earth by Hera, Zeus's lawful wife, who was a woman of unparalleled jealousy and callousness. She once even dared to steal Zeus's thunderbolt because she was so upset. The thunder god showed his wife no mercy and hung her from the sky with anvils attached to her ankles until she repented and returned the lightning bolt. After being chased around the globe by Hera, Leto finally found a place to birth her twins on the floating islands of Delos. After the birth of the twins, Hera gave up her pursuit, and Zeus gave both his children thrones on Mt. Olympus.

Like the rest of the gods and goddesses of Mt Olympus, the sun god had no shortage of lovers in his immortal life, and just like Hermes, he had an affinity for both men and women. However, most of the love myths surrounding Apollo are about women and, in particular, nymphs. One of the most famous of all myths involving Apollo was his pursuit of the Naiad nymph Daphne. One trademark of the nymphs was their ability to outrun the various gods, monsters, and creatures that sought to have or harm them. Daphne gave the sun god a good sprint, running all over Greece. Finally, in frustration, Daphne called out to Gaia to save her from Apollo's grasp. Gaia then transformed the nymph into a laurel tree. Even in her tree state, the sun god longed for her. He made the laurel wreath one of his main totems and placed laurel branches around the temple of the Oracle of Delphi.

Apollo probably had the highest number of relations with nymphs out of all the gods, and he produced some very ethereal and earthly divine children. One of the most notable is the god of olive oil, beekeeping, and the Etesian winds, Aristaeus.

Apollo was also the slayer of the mighty Python of Delphi. Sources offer contested opinions as to the origins of the great beast and its form, but what is certain is that Python was older than all the Olympians. He was a relic from the days of Chaos and the great flood. Some say that Python was one of the beasts sent by Hera to destroy Apollo's mother, Leto. Seeking revenge, Apollo shot the serpent right in the eye with one of his golden arrows. Others say that the serpent was set by Gaia to guard the Oracle of Delphi, a being of immense prophetic power. In fact, the Oracle was so powerful that she caught the attention and patronage of the sun god. The great serpent was bested with one shot from Apollo's bow, and the god usurped the patronage of Delphi.

Ares

Ares was a son that even a mother would find hard to love. He had an undeniable bloodlust, but his brutal antics suited him nicely since he was the god of war. He was not the most well-liked god of all the Olympians. Mortals feared Ares far more than they respected him. There were several deities that personified war activities, but there was nothing philosophical or redeemable about Ares's take on battles. He loved to kill for sport, desecrating and defiling the bodies of the men he fought. Despite his warlike ways, Ares has always been characterized in mythology as an irrefutable coward. And since he was the son of Zeus and Hera, he had a guaranteed throne on Olympus, unlike many other gods and goddesses.

He is usually depicted in ancient renderings as a mature man or a slender youth in full body armor. The god's seemingly one likable quality was that the god of war has never been recorded in Greek mythology as a rapist, despite the fact that rape and war always seem to pair together. He preferred a style similar to that of his father Zeus, as he had an arsenal of tricks in order to seduce mortals and immortals alike. One of Ares's most notable lovers was the goddess of love herself and the lawful wife of Hephaestus, Aphrodite. In fact, the god of blacksmiths and metallurgy, Hephaestus, caught the lovers entangled within a golden net he had made special for the occasion. He then invited the rest of the Olympians to laugh at the adulterous lovers.

From their union, the goddess of love and the god of war had four divine children: Anteros, Deimos, Phobos, and Harmonia. All of their children represented different possible outcomes or human tendencies when it comes to relationships. Anteros was the god of both unrequited and requited love. Deimos was the god of fear, while Phobos was the god of panic. Harmonia was the goddess of harmony and the mother of Semele, who would become the mother of Dionysus, the god of wine and merriment.

In addition to his warlike attributes, Ares was also the god of civil order and had a very strong sense of right and wrong. He was very protective of his loved ones, especially his children. When his daughter with Aglauros (the daughter of the king of Athens) was raped by Halirrhothius, the son of Poseidon, Ares caught the rapist in the act and slit his throat on the spot. Poseidon was outraged and brought Ares to the court of the gods to be tried as a murderer, but the gods declared by unanimous vote that Ares should be acquitted of all crimes.

By all accounts, Ares seems to be the god most invested in his children. He could be defined in modern terms as a very "hands-on father." Almost all of his children were given attention, especially if they showed promise and prowess on the battlefield. It didn't matter whether they were a boy or a girl; Ares treated all his children the same. Some of his most famous fearless sires are the Amazonian race of warrior women. Yes, the very same Amazons who would later inspire the iconic female warrior culture of Wonder Woman herself. Ares had his selected favorite daughters but doted on all the Amazons, showering them with weapons and artillery and constantly backing their war efforts. His two favorite daughters were Amazonian Queens Hippolyta and Penthesilea, to whom he gifted war belts, shields, and spears in their honor. He could definitely be considered the "dad of the year."

Eros

Eros is more commonly depicted and personified as a baby in modern representations, but his characterization in ancient Greek works of art is far more adult. He still has his signature wings, as well as his bow and arrow, but the Eros of mythology is considered to be a beautiful youth, beardless but definitely on the cusp of manhood, probably around the age of seventeen.

Some say the male god of love was the product of Aphrodite and Ares, while other myths place his origin story at the beginning of time. In this narrative, Eros is considered to be one of the original primordial beings, which would make him a sibling of Pontus, Gaia, and Erebus. They say that love makes the world go round, and it seems as if Eros has been present since the dawn of time. Since the gods and goddesses, as well as the Titans, were pursuing each other romantically since day one, it is safe to say that Eros is probably much older than the Olympians.

He is one of the more mischievous gods, as he would make mortals and immortals fall in love by shooting them with his magic love arrows. He did this mainly for sport. In fact, he was one of the more unpredictable and uncontrollable gods. Even mighty Zeus could not control the little love deviant.

For being one of the oldest forces of love in the world, Eros did not take that many lovers himself. The love story of Eros and Psyche is one of the most popularized in the world today. As the story goes, Psyche was a beautiful princess from the mortal world, the daughter of some unnamed Greek king. She was so beautiful that the men of Greece turned away from the temples of the goddess of love to worship the lovely princess. New words needed to be invented to describe the exquisite intricacies of her beauty.

Aphrodite, being Aphrodite and prone to a high degree of jealousy, did not take kindly to this. She sought to fix her Psyche problem by marrying her to the most hideous man in the world. Naturally, to make mortals magically fall in love, one would need the assistance of Eros and his magic love arrows. So, Eros flew off to do his duty for Aphrodite. However, when he came upon the princess, he was smitten by her beauty and was unable to fulfill his task. Instead, he whisked Psyche away to a secret palace, hidden far away from the sight of Aphrodite.

Psyche Revived by Cupid's Kiss *by Antonio Canova, 1787-1793.*
This work is based on a story from The Golden Ass.
(Credit: Kimberly Vardeman from Lubbock, TX, USA, CC BY 2.0
via Wikimedia Commons;
https://commons.wikimedia.org/wiki/File:Psyche_revived_by_cupid%27s_kiss,_P
aris_2_October_2011_002.jpg)

He visited her there night after night, and they lay together in sweet bliss just before the morning came. He would always leave her before the first light of day could reveal his identity. He kept this secret from her, asking that she never look upon his form and to give him her absolute trust that he was her love. Psyche and Eros were very much in love, and she was his completely, giving herself to him night after night while blindly trusting him.

Their happiness was not to last, though. Psyche's sister was jealous of her sister's contentment. She wanted to see her joy ruined, so she told Psyche that her secret love was a horrid monster, unable to be looked upon by mortal eyes.

At first, Psyche paid no mind to her sister's toxic words, but as time passed, her doubt grew stronger. Eventually, it got to be too much, and one night, she took an oil lamp and gazed at her secret love. Much to her surprise, there laid the most beautiful and desired of all the gods. Just as she was about to retreat, a drop of oil from her lamp fell and landed on his shoulder. Eros woke up in a startled daze and fled from Psyche. The poor girl was distraught. Her lack of trust had caused Eros's love and trust to flee as well. Still, she could not give him up, so she searched all of Greece for a trace of her love.

Unluckily, Psyche came upon the temple palace of Aphrodite, whose hatred and jealousy for Psyche still burned bright within her, perhaps even more so for breaking the heart of her favorite vassal. She forced the poor girl to complete a series of backbreaking and humiliating tasks. Eros, who was still deeply in love with Psyche, hid from her sight and assisted in each task so that she would be victorious and gain the favor of the goddess of love. Over time, Aphrodite came to like the girl and reunited her with Eros, who made her his wife, an immortal. She became the goddess of the soul. He bestowed upon her a pair of butterfly wings so that she would always be with him in the heavens, and they had a child named Hedone together, who was the goddess of sensual pleasure.

Hephaestus

Hephaestus's start in life was not bright or cheerful. When he was pulled from his mother, Hera, the goddess of motherhood and childbirth, she took one look at his sickly form and tossed him from the great height of Mt. Olympus. His upper body was perfectly healthy, but his legs did not seem to develop properly, and there was no room on Olympus for imperfection, at least in Hera's mind.

Hephaestus did not die when he fell to the earth, though. He was rescued by the sea goddess Thetis and her sisters and taken to their underwater grotto, where they raised him in secret, unbeknownst to his hateful mother, who presumed him to be dead. Over the years, Hephaestus's strength grew. While his lower body would always remain disabled, he built up his upper body. This strength made him the finest craftsman and metalworker in the world. He made beautiful necklaces and brooches for Thetis and her sisters, and they loved him dearly.

One day, when Thetis was sunning herself on the beach, Hera looked down from her perch in the sky and saw the beautiful jewelry adorning Thetis. She demanded that the goddess inform her where she had acquired such exquisite pieces. Thetis revealed that it was her very own abandoned son. Hera was instantly filled with regret and begged Hephaestus to return to Mt. Olympus. She offered to build him the most impressive and well-equipped workshop in all the world and give him the beautiful Aphrodite as his wife. Hephaestus accepted and returned to Olympus a prodigy. His work was the pride and beauty of Olympus. He made weapons, armor, and totems for all the gods and their children. He even made two golden women that he used to assist him in walking.

Hephaestus is also credited with being the creator of the first woman, Pandora (yes, that Pandora who unleashed all the evils onto the world), as a punishment for mankind. In the creation of mankind, Zeus was against providing man with the knowledge of fire. Prometheus, the creator of mankind, wanted more for his creations, so he stole away the secret of fire and gave it to humanity. Zeus was furious with Prometheus. He ordered the Titan to be chained to the side of a mountain in the underworld where a vulture would feast on his immortal and thus regenerating liver for all time. Who do you think made the chains that were strong enough to subdue a Titan? If you guessed Hephaestus, you would be right.

For added measure, Zeus evened the score by setting man's development back with the creation of the first woman. Legend has it that Hephaestus molded her from the clay of a riverbank, not unlike most creation myths surrounding humanity, whether those myths originated in North America or Jerusalem. He gave her bewitching features similar to that of the immortal goddesses and bestowed upon her a voice and a mind that sought to undo the spirit of man. In other words, women were the "Achilles' heel" of men.

Dionysus

The story of Greek mythology's resident god of partying and general merriment began with a high degree of death and heartbreak. Dionysus's mother, Semele, was killed while she was still pregnant. Hera saw her husband's love for the princess of Thebes and tricked Zeus into conjuring a lightning bolt that struck Semele in the chest, killing her instantly. Zeus had to act quickly if he was to save his unborn child. So, he removed the still growing fetus from Semele's womb and sewed Dionysus into his own thigh, carrying him to term. This was not the first or the last time Zeus birthed a child from his own body. Dionysus's sister Athena was born from the very skull of their father.

Hera's animosity toward Zeus's many wives and lovers could only be matched by the raw contempt she displayed toward his progeny. She continued to hunt Dionysus, who was successfully hidden for years by the satyr Silenus and his band of nymphs from Mount Nysa. It was during his time with Silenus that Dionysus first discovered the secrets of cultivating grapes for wine and taught mortals how to make the libation.

Eventually, Dionysus came to live with his aunt so he could be better protected from Hera. Semele's sister Ino and her husband Athamas welcomed Dionysus into their home. However, the joys of raising their nephew were not to last. Hera eventually found the child and his adoptive parents, and she drove Athamas to madness, causing him to murder his son and drive Ino and their other child to jump off a cliff to their deaths. (Some versions say Ino was the one to go mad.)

Needless to say, Dionysus was cast to the wind. The experience drove him mad, beginning his long history as the god of not only wine and festivities but also madness. Dionysus would do his fair share of damage to the mind of mortals throughout his tenure as an Olympian.

Before he earned his status in Olympus, he was hunted by not only immortals but also mankind. They did not respect the god of wine, and they tried to attack him and his divinity more than once. One of the main perpetrators to try such a maneuver was the king of Thebes. Dionysus retaliated by driving all of the king's daughters to madness, provoking them to rip apart their father limb from limb.

Eventually, Dionysus was welcomed back to Olympus by his father, having proved himself worthy with his ruthless yet carefree lifestyle. Dionysus adorned himself in skins and wore a wreath of vines around his head. The god of wine was constantly attended by his cult of satyrs and maenads, who were unmatched in their madness and cravings for wine, sex, hunting, and occasionally human flesh.

Dionysus himself had quite the insatiable sexual appetite and got hot for just about anything that moved. He would often get maidens and nymphs drunk and then proceeded to have his way with them. One of these rapes resulted in twins, the first of which was eaten out of sheer rage by the mother. Dionysus eventually settled down and married the princess Ariadne, who had been deserted on an abandoned island by Theseus and was later rescued by the god of wine.

Dionysus also had a few male lovers; in fact, that is where we see the more affectionate side of the god emerge. He was described as a beautiful youth and had many equally beautiful lovers. For instance, there was the young satyr Ampelos, who was killed while trying to mount a wild bull. He was added as a constellation amongst the stars by the mourning god. Ampelos became the constellation Vindemitor, the grape-picker.

Chapter Five – The Goddesses

Hera

Without a doubt, if jealousy, greed, and impulsivity had a human form, it would be the goddess Hera. She was the patron goddess of marriage, the sky, and women. She was the queen of the Olympians and a royal pain in the behind—in particular, a pain in her husband's behind. As you have probably gathered thus far, Hera could not abide the numerous affairs of her brother-husband Zeus.

While Hera was meant to be the protector of women, she had no qualms harming women she despised, usually those who fell victim to Zeus's unfaithful nature. The list of her victims is endless. Oftentimes, Zeus would transform his lovers into wild animals to save them from the wrath of his queen, but Hera was just as wily as her husband and hunted these women in both human and animal forms. In alphabetical order, these were Aegina, Elara, Iynx, Semele, and Othreis.

What's interesting is that despite her immense jealousy, she never had any affairs of her own. Incredibly enough, she stayed loyal to Zeus throughout their entire marriage. In the early years of their courtship, they were truly one of the happiest couples in the world. Their wedding was such a joyous affair that it lasted for two hundred years.

The goddess was very judgmental and often the first of the Olympians to deal out punishments to mortals and immortals alike. When Aphrodite was jumping around in one too many beds, including that of Dionysus, Adonis, and Zeus, Hera cursed her pregnancy (the identity of the father remains unknown since many different versions of the myth exist). She laid her hands on Aphrodite's swollen belly and cursed her child to be born with a bulbous form and an overly large penis. At first, Aphrodite was repulsed by her child, but it all turned out well in the end. The child, Priapus, made his gargantuan appendages work to his advantage, and he became the god of vegetable gardens, with his giant member linked to the fertility and large growth of crops. So, in the end, Hera's actions had a positive outcome, even if the intent was malicious.

She did have a few favorite heroes, with the main being Herakles, who started out as the enemy of the goddess but soon won her friendship and admiration through his heroic deeds. She actively aided in the success of Jason and the Argonauts' quest for the golden fleece. In many ways, Hera's moral compass for justice was right on target. Although this side of Hera wasn't seen as often as her vengeful side, she had a fervor for the pursuit of justice that matched her beauty. This goddess didn't back down for anything or anyone.

The Greek king of the Lapiths, Ixion, once dared to cross the goddess by attempting to rape her. She escaped the grasp of King Ixion and took the matter to her lord and husband, Zeus. Zeus would not convict this man without concrete proof of his crimes, so Zeus sought to entrap Ixion and crafted a cloud from the heavens to take the shape of Hera. Ixion overtook the cloud and bragged that he had his way with the goddess, which, whether he had or had not, was not a great thing to boast about since Zeus would undoubtedly hear. Zeus then apprehended him and tied him to an ever-turning wheel in the sky.

Demeter

Demeter was the goddess of agriculture and, more specifically, grains. She is often depicted as an older woman bearing bundles of wheat with a golden crown laid upon her head. She sustained the earth with her bounty, and for this reason, she wielded a tremendous amount of power and influence amongst the Olympians. When her anger flared, she didn't hesitate to cause a famine. In fact, her main weapon of punishment was to cause mortals to feel immense hunger. This was her sentence for Erysichthon, who dared to incite the anger of Demeter by cutting down the goddess's holy grove.

Like a true mother, Demeter showed a great deal of favor and care to all mankind. She took many demi-gods under her wing whom she found to be worthy of her patronage. One of these heroes was Triptolemos. He was an Eleusinian prince who hosted the goddess Demeter most graciously when her daughter Persephone went missing, during which time she went scouring the earth for nine days, imbibing no nectar or ambrosia. Triptolemos offered Demeter comforting words, which encouraged her to pursue her search for her most beloved child. As a reward for his heart and hospitality, Demeter taught him the ways of cultivating grain and made him a herald unto man so that he could deliver the secrets of the earth to every household. This was an immense honor and responsibility; the Titans and other gods had not even been afforded such trust and confidence. She even gifted a golden-winged chariot to Triptolemos so that he could carry her gifts across the world with great ease.

Demeter had a fair number of lovers in her lifetime but far less than that of her brothers and other goddesses. She took a romantic liking to mortals more for who they were as people rather than their legendary good looks or meager deeds. The only immortal consensual lover she took was her brother Zeus, which resulted in the birth of the goddess and queen of the underworld, Persephone.

Although Hera was Zeus's true wife, he always carried a deep love for his sister Demeter and was known to strike down her lovers with extreme jealousy and prejudice. This is what befell poor Iasion, a prince of the island of Crete. He slept with the goddess in a plowed field and was killed almost instantly by Zeus's thunderbolt. However, Zeus did not get there fast enough, and Iasion impregnated Demeter with twin sons, Plutus and Philomelos.

There indeed was something about Demeter because almost all of her brothers were either interested in sleeping with her or marrying her offspring. Poseidon, true to his nature, even raped his own sister. Legend has it that Poseidon pursued Demeter with relentless "passion" while she was searching for Persephone. This moment was one of the lowest and most vulnerable in the goddess's history. In an attempt to escape Poseidon's grasp, Demeter transformed herself into a mare and started to graze in an open field. Poseidon was not so easily fooled and came up from behind her as a stallion and took her forcefully. From this union, the immortal horse Arion was born. He would become the mount for many prominent heroes, including Oncius and Herakles.

Hestia

Hestia was the firstborn child of Cronos and Rhea; therefore, she was the first to be swallowed and the last to be regurgitated. Without a doubt, Hestia seemed to be the most inherently talented and assured out of all her siblings. The other original Olympians and, for that matter, the later generations as well, could all be insecure, jealous, and dependent on one another and mortals for assurance of their divinity. Hestia never behaved in such a manner, and from the start, she seemed to possess a wisdom and self-awareness uncommon amongst the gods and even the Titans. Her physical appearance is thought to be that of an older woman. She is typically veiled and holds a kettle.

There were several virgin goddesses amongst the Olympians, but the first was Hestia, who was the goddess of the hearth and the home. She provided light during the night in every home across Greece. The warmth that stems from her is not only a physical light but also an emotional light. Hestia's fire was what cooked the meals of the world and thus brought humanity together. Meals and drinking were some of Greece's largest camaraderie activities, so naturally, the goddess of the hearth was very highly venerated among the various cults of Greece.

The link between Hestia and fire is the concept of transformation. Symbols and substances were consumed and then transformed in the fire. This meant that some of the sacrifices dedicated to the gods by fire were dedicated in honor of Hestia. Without her, Greek worship would have been meaningless, regardless of whether the worship was directed toward the other gods and goddesses. "Among mortal men she was the chief of the goddesses."[1]

Although the myths surrounding the goddess are few, Hestia has quite a few hymns dedicated in her honor. She was hailed as one of the most respected and honored of the Olympians, with her vow of chastity protected and enforced by the king of the gods himself. Even Poseidon opted for a more dignified approach in his pursuance of Hestia. Instead of heading right for his rapist tendencies, he asked Zeus for her hand in marriage. He was, of course, denied, and Hestia was given watch over the divine hearth in Olympus.

There was one other incident in the goddess's romantic history where her chastity was almost overtaken. The fair Titan and mother to the Olympians, Rhea, was hosting a banquet for all the illustrious and divine immortals of the world. Gods, nymphs, satyrs, and spirits

---

[1] Homeric Hymn 5 to Aphrodite 18 ff (trans. Evelyn-White) (Greek epic circa 7th–4th BCE).

alike attended her festival, which had no shortage of wine. Fair Hestia laid her head down on the ground for a short spell in order to rest. In her innocence, she never suspected she was being watched by another. Priapus (if you can recall, he was the god of vegetable gardens with the enormous appendage) saw the figure of a female resting on the ground. Whether he knew it was the goddess or some random woodland nymph is still debated. However, he approached her with lust and sought to force himself upon her. Just as he was about to pounce, a donkey that was tied to a tree nearby let out a giant bray, startling the goddess awake. She screamed at the sight of Priapus's huge member, thus alerting the party guests to the situation. Priapus fled before they all arrived, but his name carried great shame from that day forward. This was likely because Hestia was highly revered by gods and mortals alike.

Athena

Athena can be best thought of as the woman prepared for any and all situations. She was the patron goddess of wisdom, arts and crafts, battle strategy, weaving, and pottery, and she was the patron goddess of heroes. Her identification with war is wholly different from that of her brother Ares. Athena saw war as a time for men to show that their wits could win the day, not brawn and muscle. The goddess could hold her own in battle and once engaged in a fight with the god of war, Ares, in which she triumphed. For this reason, the heroes who she took under her wing usually were the brightest, smartest, and most curious among men. Think of Odysseus, who was arguably her favorite man among mortals.

She was also the most credited Olympian when it came to teaching a variety of skills to the human race. She even beat out her uncle Poseidon for the patronage of Athens, the most innovative and progressive Greek *polis*. As the legend goes, the gods entered into a competition of gifts to see who could provide the most well-liked gift to the people of Athens. Poseidon provided the people with a whole sea, where they could fish and ride the waves to find new islands. Athena decided to plant an olive tree for the people. The gods and men judged that Athena was the victor, and ever since then, the tree of life, the olive tree, has grown strong on the Acropolis. Some even say that when the Persians conquered Athens, they laid waste Athena's tree. The next day, the tree grew back, doubling its height in the process.

There are very few moments in Greek mythology in which Athena does not succeed in her endeavors. Ever since her birth, she was ready for action, and it was the very circumstances surrounding her birth that made her one of the most famous and beloved of all the gods and goddesses of Mt. Olympus.

Athena's mother was the immortal Titan Metis, the patron divine being of kingly wisdom and council. She was the first official wife of Zeus, and as such, Zeus found her to be his most trusted confidant and right-hand woman in all matters. She was clever—maybe too clever. Zeus was indeed his father's son and feared that Metis or her offspring might hold more favor with the gods and humanity and, therefore, usurp his throne one day. Heeding the advice of Gaia, Zeus devoured his wife so that her powers of determining between good and evil with ease would seep into his own consciousness.

However, the great Zeus did not know that Metis was with child. At the end of Athena's gestation period, Zeus developed a horrible splitting headache. The pain was far greater than anything the god had ever experienced before. He was in so much pain that he called for Hephaestus and begged him to open his head up with his mighty ax so that whatever was in there might escape and provide him some relief. Hephaestus was reluctant, but he did as Zeus commanded. He swung his ax high and brought the blade crashing down on Zeus's skull. Out sprang Athena, fully armed with a spear, shield, and helmet. There were no first steps or childhood for Athena; she was born grown. She instantly had a deep sense of autonomy, her father's relentless spirit, and her mother's views on right and wrong.

Pottery depicting the birth of Athena from Zeus's forehead, c. 570–560 BCE.
(Public Domain,
https://commons.wikimedia.org/wiki/File:Exaleiptron_birth_Athena_Louvre_CA 616_n2.jpg)

Athena was far too busy in her self-improvement and that of humanity to develop any kind of sexual desire for mankind. She viewed them as her students, not her playthings, but she also did not seek the attention of any immortal either. She was, of course, a beautiful, stately goddess, but she found the whole idea of coitus to be revolting. One of the most well-known myths about her repulsion to sex is the transformation of Medusa. Medusa, the Gorgon from the story of Perseus, was once a beautiful maiden (she is also characterized as a nymph in some versions). She came from the island of Kisthene, which was somewhere in the Red Sea. She was so lovely that she tempted the god Poseidon, and it is no surprise that the god of the roaring seas came to overtake her.

The story goes that Medusa attempted to hide in the shrine of the virgin goddess but was unsuccessful. Poseidon followed her there and took her on the hard marble floor. The goddess tried to cover her eyes with her shield, but she was unable to remove herself from their presence. While some would think the goddess would feel sympathy and heartache for the maiden, her initial reaction was nothing but disgust. Athena knew what to do to fix this issue of Medusa's beauty. She transformed her into a hideously scaled monster, with snakes for hair and a gaze that would turn any living thing of flesh and blood to stone. This snake became one of Athena's primary symbols and can be seen decorating her armor.

Aphrodite

Aphrodite was the goddess of love and beauty, the famed Venus de Milo, an inspiration for a million and one women throughout history, and, without a doubt, one of the most villainous of all the goddesses. The beauty of Aphrodite was inhuman (literally since she was birthed from the sea foam where the testicles of Uranus had been discarded). In most classical Greek art renderings and pottery, she is shown without clothing, making her the ultimate symbol of body positivity in Greek and Roman culture. The Greeks marveled at the beauty of the human form every chance they got, which was one of the main reasons that the ancient Greek Olympics were held entirely in the nude.

Naturally, the goddess of love and beauty was unmatched in charms and her looks, right? Wrong! Although Aphrodite was considered to be the fairest amongst all the goddesses and mortals alike, her personality was not; at times, she was the antithesis of sexuality, self-sufficiency, and confidence. No one likes a jealous partner. And like Hera, Aphrodite had enough jealousy and insecurity to last her several immortal lifespans. She was quick to punish those who questioned her beauty or matchmaking abilities. For this reason, she had a great dislike of the virgin goddesses— Athena, Artemis, and Hestia. She was deeply hurt that these women found her position on Olympus to be a waste of time.

Although Aphrodite was a very vain goddess, she had a soft spot for men and women desperate for love. Everyone deserves companionship, but for some, it is harder to find. One of the more positive myths surrounding Aphrodite was her favor and patronage of the king of Kypros (Cyprus), Pygmalion. The king had taken his throne as a celibate man, and no matter how hard he or his court tried, they could not seem to arrange a marriage. The king was a gentle soul that any woman would be fortunate enough to call her own, but alas, he remained single and in a state of perpetual loneliness. That is until the goddess took pity upon him. She had heard the prayers of Pygmalion and sought to find him a match at the first opportunity.

She could have sent her son Eros to bewitch one of the many ladies of the kingdom to love the king, but she didn't feel the need to resort to such an action. The king would provide his own template for the ideal lover in the form of an ivory statue. This lonely king had quite the artistic nature and had worked for many moons on a statue of incomparable beauty, one filled with curves. He laid with this statue every night, caressing her as if she were a real woman. This may sound a little off and strange, but one shouldn't be so quick to judge, considering all the modern methods humans use to get aroused these days.

Then came the festival of Aphrodite, in which many bulls were sacrificed in honor of the goddess. Her spirit was present at each and every one of these banquets. When the king stepped forward to make his offering, he prayed to the goddess of love and asked her to send him a woman likened to that of his beloved marble lady. Aphrodite heard the king's meaningful and sincere prayers, and she was all too happy to oblige.

Instead of sending a woman born of flesh and blood, the goddess did one better. Pygmalion returned to his bed that night to lay once more with the marble woman. As he was resting his head upon her bare bosom, he noticed that her chest seemed to rise and fall. The king quickly brushed the thought aside, knowing that such things were impossible. Yet the breathing continued, and when he went to take her hand, he felt the warmth and softness of human skin. He raised his head, and his eyes met that of a maiden's, young and bashful. The king lay with his ideal love the whole night, giving thanks to the goddess for finally bringing him his perfect love and ultimate bliss.

Artemis

The last of the virgin goddesses was Artemis. She was seen as forever young, beautiful, and chaste. She was the huntress of the night, the lady of the moon, the twin sister of Apollo, and the patron goddess of young girls. Artemis commanded the entire respect of Olympus and the mortal world. Without a doubt, she was one of her father's favorite daughters; anything Artemis asked for, she received. Upon her request, Zeus gifted two golden bows and arrows to her and her brother so that they might hunt together. He also fulfilled many other divine requests from his young daughter, such as making her goddess of the dawn and the crop-killing frost, as well as making the stormy mountains her hunting domain.

From day one, her precocious nature was evident when shortly after her own birth, she assisted her mother, Leto, in delivering Apollo. This made her the goddess of childbirth. She worked closely with Hera, who was the patron mother goddess of women and child labor. While she was the protector of young children, Artemis was also tasked with bringing sudden death and disease to young female infants. Her twin brother Apollo had the same charge but for all the male babies of Greece.

Unlike the other virgin goddesses, who were usually depicted as mature women, Artemis never seemed to age past what Vladimir Nabokov (the writer of *Lolita*) would have termed a "nymphette." She was seen as a young girl just on the cusp of womanhood but still young enough to be considered a sexual innocent. She is rarely ever seen without her crescent moon crown, and she is typically flanked by a faun or buck. She is also always seen with her bow and quiver. Artemis is the natural world personified. She was both nurturing and cruel, wild yet orderly, and she was always quick to provide for others when she felt that they were deserving.

Artemis, like her sister Athena, had very little fear of confrontation and battle. For instance, she and her brother Apollo slew the giant Python that had been sent by Hera to torment their mother, Leto. In defense of her virginity, she was unparalleled in her ruthlessness. Actaeon, a young prince of Thebes, once came upon the goddess bathing and dared to steal a peek at her naked form. The goddess felt so violated and disrespected that she transformed the young prince into a stag and set his own dogs on him. They ripped him voraciously limb from limb. She exacted similar punishments on any man who dared violate her chastity, even if it was only with their eyes.

Artemis rarely kept company with the other gods and goddesses of Olympus, save for her brother. Most of the time, she preferred to keep to the company of wild animals and a select entourage of maiden attendants she protected with the fervor of a mother bear. She loved them, and they loved her. When one of them fell from grace and succumbed to the temptations of sex, Artemis was quick to exact punishment, although these punishments were far more merciful than other pettier immortals. It has been told that one of her maidens, Callisto, fell prey to the charms of Zeus and became pregnant with his child. When Artemis discovered that her own father had deflowered one of her maidens, she went ballistic. In her rage, she transformed Callisto into a large bear and sent her away into the wilderness to deliver her child. Later, when the goddess took her bow to go hunting, she came upon the bear. She did not recognize that it was Callisto, and she fired her weapon. Callisto was killed instantly. When Artemis discovered the truth, she was filled with unbearable remorse. So, she cast the figure of Callisto in her bear form into the stars to become the constellation of Ursa Major.

Persephone

It was said that Persephone was such a radiant beauty that all the gods of Olympus made Demeter offers for her hand in marriage, including Poseidon, Ares, and Apollo. Her mother would accept none of these offers, for her love for Persephone was too great to ever part with the sweet child. Persephone was also highly favored among her other chaste siblings, in particular Athena. The two half-sisters were raised together on the same island, and they would pick flowers together for hours on end.

The most famous myth surrounding Persephone is her abduction and rape by her husband/uncle Hades. He also fell instantly in love the moment he saw Persephone. The god of the underworld was a perpetually gloomy figure, so when Zeus saw his fondness for the girl, he gifted Persephone to Hades as his bride in order to ease his loneliness. Perhaps he felt guilty for his brother living in exile amongst the dark depths of the earth. However, Zeus knew that Demeter would not separate willingly from her daughter, and so he instructed Hades to abduct Persephone when she and Demeter least expected it.

The Rape of Proserpina *by Gian Lorenzo Bernini, 1621–1622.*
(Credit: Gian Lorenzo Bernini, CC BY-SA 4.0 ,
via Wikimedia Commons;
https://commons.wikimedia.org/wiki/File:Rape_of_Prosepina_September_2015-3a.jpg)

One day, when Persephone was gathering flowers in a field near her mother, Hades rode up from a dark crack in the earth. He snatched her up in his chariot and dragged her down to his kingdom. Demeter was furious and scoured the earth for her daughter. For nine days, the goddess wandered the earth, enduring all sorts of mistreatment at the hands of the other gods. She didn't eat or drink any nectar or ambrosia for this entire period either. When she discovered that Persephone had been taken by her brother, she approached Zeus on Mt. Olympus and demanded the release of her daughter. Zeus would not oblige, so Demeter caused a famine and scourge on all the animals, forests, and fields.

Eventually, a bargain was made in order to save humanity so that they would not starve. Zeus commanded Hades to release Persephone back to Demeter, but her daughter could not leave. In the early days of Persephone's captivity, she would not eat or drink anything out of protest. She was eventually tricked into eating a few seeds from a pomegranate, the fruit of the dead. Once a soul had eaten the food of the dead, they could never depart the underworld.

The gods were able to meet halfway on this one. Persephone was permitted to emerge from the underworld for one season to spend with her mother. She would, however, be required to return to the underworld once her time was up. The time of year when Persephone returned to the land of the living was when the first light and vegetation of spring break through the cold of winter and snow. When she was below the surface, the world darkened due to her mother's sadness and grief.

Chapter Six – The Gigantomachy

Let's take a step back now. The Olympians had cast down the reign of their father Cronos and imprisoned his siblings in tormenting punishments that would be carried out until the end of time. Although Gaia had called for the removal of her son from the throne of the world, she was not content with the punishments bestowed on the rest of her children. In fact, she scoffed at the greed of the Olympians. These children were no different or better than her son or her husband before him. These gods were not worthy to rule over the heavens and the earth. Their actions greatly offended Gaia, and she proclaimed in her frustration, "Have they forgotten to revere the earth, their mother?"

From her bitterness, she gave birth to a new race of children from the deepest underbellies of Tartarus, a race of giants, large, brooding, lawless, and lethal. Many sources describe the giants as being clad in shining armor, with beards and hair that brushed the floor. Their lower bodies were covered in scales, and they are sometimes referred to as the scaly sons of Gaia. They stood between nine and twelve cubits high, at least according to the Greek 5th-century epic composed by Nonnus of Panopolis. The height of one cubit is about forty-five centimeters or one and a half feet, making each giant thirteen feet or taller. These giants had grown in the deep womb of their mother, and they had been sired by Uranus himself. When Cronos had castrated his father and tossed his genitals into the sea, there were several other divine specimens that resulted from this action. There was Aphrodite, who grew from the testicles themselves; the Furies, goddesses of vengeance; and the giants (sometimes referred to as Gigantes). This specific generation of giants was known as the Thracian giants, so named for the location of their birth.

Gaia stirred up the giants to war by proclaiming that they needed to avenge her and the Titans by overthrowing Olympus. They needed to cast down Poseidon and put him in chains at the bottom of the sea and rip out Apollo's golden curls. Typhoeus, the great unclean serpent, could take control of Zeus's thunderbolt, and these beastly giants could claim the goddesses for themselves and jest about the rape of Athena, Artemis, and Aphrodite. The giants were crazed and enraged by the poisonous words of their mother, so much so that they already thought themselves the victors. They began to hurl stones and flaming oak trees at the gates of heaven and tormented mankind, attempting to provoke the Olympians to war. Little did they know they would be in for one of the greatest battles of their time.

Zeus sent out one of his most trusted messengers, Iris, and she convened a council of the immortals from every corner of the world in order to aid the gods in their battle. Even Hades and his queen, Persephone, emerged from their dark dwelling place to defend the existence of Olympus. When all the immortals had gathered, Zeus addressed them all with a war speech. The following excerpt is translated from Hesiod's *Theogony*.

"Deathless army, whose dwelling-place is, and must ever be, the sky, ye whom no adverse fortune can ever harm, mark ye how Earth with her new children conspires against our kingdom and undismayed has given birth to another brood? Wherefore, for all the sons she bore, let us give back to their mother as many dead; let her mourning last through the ages as she weeps by as many graves as she now has children."

The war is thought to have taken place on the plains of Phlegra, but some believe that it occurred in Thrace, which was the original birthplace of the giants. There is also a historical and cultural connection to be highlighted with this location. The Thracian tribes that existed north of Greece were considered to be barbaric in comparison to the sophisticated Greek civilization. Thus, these tribes' lawlessness is metaphorically attached to a race of vengeful and jealous abominations.

When the war kicked off, nature was drastically thrown off balance. Each time the gods were provoked, there was an equal and opposite reaction in the natural world. Rivers changed their direction, mountains collapsed, and huge swells flooded the land. In addition to this, the giants also armed themselves with the elements of their mother Gaia in order to defeat the great weapons of the gods. There was very little that could rival the craftsmanship of the gods' Cyclopes-forged weapons, but the giants were still coming for them, strapped for battle. They hurled great mountains and entire islands against the gods. It was nothing for them to grab an island right out of the sea and hurl it toward the heavens. The entirety of the earth was in disarray, but the battle still raged on, with each god and goddess contributing to a great and bloody victory. However, the most referenced Olympians in the Gigantomachy are Zeus, Athena, Ares, and Hera. There is also special attention paid to the mortal allies of the gods in this war, particularly the hero Herakles.

The entire atmosphere of the battlefield was clouded, as it was filled with the dust of ancient mountains and ash. There was so much disarray that it was hard to tell the difference between the two armies. Still, Ares was the first to charge into the fray, his shield and breastplate glistening red, his helmet sitting high on his brow. With a mighty swing of his sword, he cleaved into the giant Pelorus's groin, tearing him from stem to stern. He then proceeded to ride over the dismembered figure of the giant until his wheels slid slick across the earth with blood and ripped flesh.

Athena also showed no hesitation in joining the battle. True to her nature, she was able to defeat her enemies with very little energy and a great deal of finesse. During this battle, Athena wore the Gorgon Medusa's head on her own breastplate. She knew this would be enough to stop anything in her path. She stood steadfast, with her spear and shield calmly reserved at her side as she thrust her breast forward. The giant Pallas was the first to be turned to stone. Fear gripped him, and he exclaimed, "What is this icy feeling that grips my limbs?" He dropped to his knees with a groan, which was soon turned into rock. In frustration over the loss of two of his brothers, one of the giants heaved his brother's stone corpse at Athena. She stepped to the side with the same ease as before, and Pallas exploded on the mountain behind her.

There is another version of Pallas's death that is just as riveting. In a blind rage, he charged the goddess, careful to turn his eyes to the side as he did so to avert his gaze from the petrifying stare of the Gorgon. Athena was not fazed. With a swing of her shield, she deflected the blow of the giant while simultaneously bringing her sword from underneath. With one great swipe, she cleaved off the giant's right arm. With this deathly blow, he let his gaze slip and caught the eyes of Athena's breastplate. This finished the giant for good.

Athena could not be stopped in her defense of Olympus. Her most heroic act came when she managed to bury the giant Enceladus underneath Mt. Etna. To this day, Enceladus remains there, generating the volcanic lava that stirs within.

The remainder of the Olympians disposed of the remaining giants. Artemis, seeking to defend her honor, which had been offended by the blasphemies of the giants, flew into battle armed with her bow and arrow. She slew the giant Aigaion. Her brother and Herakles, one of the greatest heroes among men, slaughtered the giant Ephialtes. Apollo sent an arrow soaring into the giant's left eye while Herakles took the right. Hephaestus bested the giant Mimas by hurling hot molten iron into his face.

Poseidon pursued Polybotes throughout the seas and finally managed to run him down at the island of Nisyros. Poseidon broke a piece of the island and threw it at Polybotes. The chunk of the island came in contact with the giant's torso, crushing his organs and killing him instantly. Hermes, who was armed with Hades's helmet of invisibility, bested the giant Hippolytus in his wily fashion. He swung his mighty sword and, with a few blows, cleaved Hippolytus in half. Dionysus, armed only with his thyrsus (a staff or wand wrapped in vines with a fennel cone mounted on the top, typically used in Hellenistic cult rituals), killed the giant Eurytus.

An image on a cup dated to the late 5th century BCE that shows Poseidon attacking Polybotes, with Gaia in the background.

(Credit: Sailko, CC BY 3.0, via Wikimedia Commons;

https://commons.wikimedia.org/wiki/File:Aristophanes,_kylix_attica_con_giganto machia,_410_ac_ca._02.JPG)

Herakles also managed to destroy the only immortal among the race of giants: Alkyoneus. As long as he remained within the confines of his ancestral homeland, the plains of Pallene, he could not be wounded or killed. He was considered to be the king of the giants, along with his brother Porphyrion. Athena found a loophole around Alkyoneus's immortality. After Herakles fired countless arrows into the giant's torso, Athena advised him to drag Alkyoneus beyond the border of the plains so that he could perish in agony. Herakles also killed the giant Leon and skinned him in order to fashion a protective cloak from his rock-hard exterior. Athena did the same with the skin of her victim Pallas.

The Fates managed to take care of a few of the beastly giants and disposed of Agrios and Thoon, beating them to death with bronze maces. Even the race of immortal horses born of the wind and ocean immortals lent their hand in the battle to destroy the giants. Some, of course, sided with the usurpers. These were Xanthus and Balius, who would become the horses of the tragic hero Achilles.

It was these immortals and those born of mortal women who fought for Zeus in the war of the gods that received the title Olympian if it had not already been bestowed upon them. Of course, Zeus was the most impressive immortal in the Gigantomachy, as he brought an end to the most powerful of the giant race, Porphyrion. When Porphyrion rushed to rape Zeus's wife and queen Hera, the god of the skies hurled thunderbolt after thunderbolt directly at the giant, who was struck dead by these blows.

During the Gigantomachy, there was plenty of treachery against the king of the gods. Zeus had few allies but numerous enemies, even those he considered to be his friends. This included Olympos, a giant of reason who raised Zeus and taught him the order of law and the secrets of the earth. Olympos betrayed Zeus by supporting the giants in their revolt against the gods. This was devastating for Zeus, and in his anger, he struck down Olympos. He was so grieved over the death of his foster-father that he built Olympos a great tomb and named the resting place after himself so that people would think it was the grave of Zeus, causing it to always be visited and revered. The only giant to survive the war was Aristaeus. He was spirited away to the island of Sicily by Gaia and transformed into a dung beetle so that he could be hidden from the gods.

Chapter Seven – Typhoeus

Typhoeus was a volcano demon. His weapons of choice were great smoldering volcanic rocks that he hurled at Olympus, and from his mouth poured the endless fires that were stored at the center of the earth. There is much debate around the parentage of the greatest of calamities and the father of all monsters. Some say he was the accursed child of Hera, born from her rage at Zeus for having given birth to Athena.

Hera, true to form, did not take her husband's newest "offense" lying down. She beset the help of Gaia and the great underworld to grant her a child that would not be Zeus's. She asked that Mother Gaia give her child the strength to defeat the king of the gods and be sent as a plague to torment mankind. Gaia was moved by her pleas and fulfilled her request. Queen Hera did not visit the bed of her husband for a full year, not that he seemed to care or notice (he had plenty of other prospects to keep him distracted). At the end of that year, she labored greatly to birth the monster of all monsters, and from then on, fear reigned throughout the world, even at the heights of Olympus.

Some other sources say he was born from the depths of Tartarus and that he was Gaia's last-ditch effort to overthrow the Olympians. Typhoeus took the shape of a collection of some of the most powerful and terrifying animals in nature. His lower half was that of a snake, with multiple long scaly bodies. These led into the torso of a man, but this was where Typhoeus's link to mankind or any kind of humanity ended. From his back sprouted two great wings that easily blew away the clouds and cleared trees from the land with one quick flap. His hair and beard hung heavy in large and stinking smoky mats. His eyes glowed red with the fire of the underworld, and his ears came to sharp points at the top, which were just as serrated and dangerous as his gnashing teeth.

The strength of Typhoeus was unrivaled in the world of Greek mythology. Even Zeus had his fears and doubts about his abilities to defeat Typhoeus. His head passed the great clouds, and his serpent tails gripped and warped the earth. His voice bellowed and growled from deep within him, as would a lion or a bull as they built up to attack. It was said that his war cry was the cry of all these beasts put together, along with a soft chorus of hisses.

Typhoeus is known as the father of all monsters. With the great serpent maiden Echidna, the pair managed to conceive some of the most feared and respected monsters among men and gods. These children feature prominently in other tales, often being cast in the standard role of "Greek hero's opponent" or, better yet, "creature to be slain in order to prove one's worth to a bunch of whiny immortals." Oftentimes, these monsters never instigated the fight. However, the children of Typhoeus and Echidna also birthed some monster babies that caused serious drama. So, villainy was definitely a family affair in Greek mythology.

The first child that Echidna bore was Orthros, the hound of the giant Geryon. Orthros was a two-headed dog with a serpent tail. Orthros was tasked with guarding the red cattle of Geryon on the island of Erytheia. He was ferocious and dedicated to his mission. He was slain by the hero Herakles, who was sent to fetch one of these prized cattle as one of his twelve labors. In the process, Orthros's master was also slain. Not all of Typhoeus's children pursued evil day and night; some were just average monsters committed to the task with which they had been charged.

From Typhoeus's union with Echidna also emerged the most famous employee of Hades and the guardian of the gates of the underworld: Cerberus. This monster ate raw flesh and had three ferocious heads that swiveled and snapped in every direction. He prevented souls from escaping their fate in the dark depths of the earth. However, he could be bested with teamwork. Just like Orthros, Herakles was also charged with the capture of Cerberus as one of his twelve labors. He was successful only with the help of the queen of the underworld, Persephone, and the bright-eyed Athena. It was an inside job with the logistics of the smartest strategist on Olympus, possibly the world.

Their third child, the Hydra, was born of the great serpent but nourished at the breast of Queen Hera. The milk of the goddess fueled a monstrous and highly formidable beast that stalked the swamps of Lerna. Best described as a "drakonian serpent" by Stephen of Byzantium, the Hydra had a very special regenerative feature to its body, making the monster hard to wound and kill. The beast had nine heads, with eight mortal ones and one immortal, which was the head that rested in the middle. Every time it lost a head, one grew in its place. This was a skill discovered by (you guessed it) none other than Herakles.

Typhoeus was also the father of the Chimera, a fire-breathing monster with three different animal heads. The middle head was a lion, the right one was a dragon or serpent, and the left head was a goat. All these heads were attached to the body of a lion and finished with the classic Greek mythology monster tail, which took the form of a snake. It also had a goat's udder located underneath its rear end. The Chimera would become the mother of other famous monsters, such as the Sphinx and the Nemean lion.

The emergence of Typhoeus from the underbelly of the earth was a clear sign of attack. Zeus and the rest of the gods knew that this new beast would eventually show up at the gates of Olympus. The Olympians fled to Egypt and transformed into animals in order to hide from Typhoeus. He was so ferocious and blood-crazed that the gods feared for their immortal souls. Well, all of them but Zeus, who sought to act first before Typhoeus struck with his fury. Zeus knew that if the monster began developing his raging momentum that he would not be able to stop him.

Zeus called to Hephaestus and ordered the smith of the gods to forge thunderbolts of considerable strength and energy for him. Hephaestus took to this task day and night. Zeus then began his battle with the great Typhoeus, striking him with repeated thunderbolts, weakening his spirit and buying the king of the gods time to decide how to best defeat the beast for good. Zeus then hurled the strongest bolt deep into the sea, splitting open the earth and causing the hot fire from its core to melt away the layers until the gaping mouth of Tartarus was revealed. With a final blow, Zeus managed to back Typhoeus into the pit, and he sealed the crack in the ocean floor, locking the father of monsters away in the dark for all eternity.

According to tradition, Typhoeus still has some influence over the winds of the earth and particularly the seas. From his prison beneath the crusts of the planet, he is able to cause cataclysmic events, such as land swells and rogue waves that send sailors and fishermen to their deaths.

Greek pottery with a depiction of Zeus throwing one of his thunderbolts at Typhoeus. Public Domain,

https://commons.wikimedia.org/wiki/File:Zeus_Typhon_Staatliche_Antikensam mlungen_596.jpg

Chapter Eight – The Creation of Man, the Flood, the New Generation, and Women as the Curse of Mankind

When the time came for the creation of mankind, the task was appointed to the Titan who had fought with the Olympians to defeat Cronos: Prometheus. While there were other Titans that stood with Zeus in the battle for the throne of the world, Prometheus was the most trusted of his generation. Zeus gave him a second-in-command, his brother Epimetheus, to complete the task of making all mortal creatures, human beings and animals alike. Epimetheus was the Titan of afterthought and excuses. He was the son of Iapetus and Clymene and the husband of the first woman ever created. Her storyline is very similar to the biblical Eve. This was none other than Pandora. In both these stories, women were blamed for releasing the negative aspects of creation onto humanity.

Epimetheus and Prometheus were by no means perfect with their own creations. In fact, they upset Zeus a great deal with how they chose to handle the creation of mortals. Both animals and men were fashioned from the same base: a little bit of clay and some water for shaping. This is not dissimilar to other creation myths. It mimics the biblical narrative, as well as a few indigenous legends. When it came to the individualization of men and animals, Epimetheus was not thinking clearly and gave all of the predatory physical qualities to the animals and beasts. He bestowed upon them long claws to defend themselves and to tear into flesh. He also gave them thick fur and scales to protect them from the elements. He made their sense of smell and taste heightened, and he made their eyes glow in the dark. These frightening little lights in the night would plague the dreams of men.

Essentially, men were left shivering and bald in the winds of the world. This simply would not do. Prometheus was willing to go to extreme lengths in order to preserve the dignity and overall happy existence of humanity. So, for men's comfort and pleasure, he stole the knowledge and prowess of the mechanical arts from Hephaestus, along with a piece of the divine flame from his workshop. He also took the knowledge of crafts and intellect from the goddess Athena. Prometheus gifted these to humanity so that they might warm their houses, cook their food, and work their metals. They could now fashion weapons and protect themselves from the beats that Epimetheus had so fervently armored.

When Zeus heard what Prometheus had done, he was enraged. It was not the fact that Prometheus had stolen intellectual and physical properties from not one but two Olympians, but it was what he did with those gifts. Zeus had a very tumultuous relationship with humanity. In fact, before Prometheus's draft of mankind, there were other kinds that came before. These beings were created by the Titans, mainly by the hands of Cronos and his brothers. This was the first generation of mankind known as the gold generation. These beings wanted for nothing and were considered to be perfect.

But they were maybe a little too perfect. The Greek theologian Hesiod considered these beings to be immortal. In fact, he believed that Cronos fashioned their body composition in a way that allowed them to age backward. When they were at the end of their days, these beings did not know pain or strife. They simply reverted to their original spirit form and roamed the earth as demons. When the reign of the Titans and Cronos came crashing down, so, too, came the end of the line of the golden generation because they would not worship the Olympian order. In all honesty, they probably considered themselves to be equal heirs of Cronos since they had been his most prized creations. They likely would have thought themselves better than his actual children. And why not? They were perfect beings, after all.

There were several generations of men before the generation created by Prometheus, Epimetheus. The next generation after the golden beings was aptly named the silver generation of humanity. These beings were the creations of Zeus, and to make sure history would remember his insecure daddy issues, Zeus made sure that this generation was physically and intellectually inferior to the Olympians. These humans were not only ugly and dumb but also bored. The only task that Zeus bestowed upon them was the worship of the gods and the planting of grain. In the end, the silver generation refused to pay the gods the homage they thought they deserved, and Zeus ended up terminating the entire race and sending them to Hades to become blessed spirits of the underworld. How blessed was this, though?

The generation that came after silver was naturally bronze. The third generation, the bronze generation, was even more lackluster than the silver generation. Zeus created these humans out of ash trees. They were warlike, exclusively carnivorous, and very capable smiths, building their houses and weapons solely out of bronze. Their chief characteristic was that they were prone to quick and emotional decision-making. Over time, this began to annoy Zeus.

He hated his creation for the very thing he created them for, to be simplistic and subservient beings incapable of evolving. This generation was satisfactory to the gods until they weren't, as they would eventually cause wars and riots, being too stupid to see that they brought the most suffering upon themselves. Zeus thus brought about a great deluge and flooded the world in order to rid the land of these brainless human beings.

The only two survivors of the great flood were the northern Greek king of Thessaly, Deucalion, and his wife, Pyrrha. Deucalion was the son of the Titan Prometheus, and his father managed to warn him of Zeus's plans to flood the world. In the classical and biblical fashion, Deucalion constructed an ark in order to save himself and his wife from the rising waters. They were washed on top of Mount Parnassus. There, they fathered the Hellenic human race by casting stones behind them as they made their way up the mountain, as instructed by the god Hermes.

After that came the final generation of men, the men created by the hands of the Titans instead of the gods. The truth of the matter was that the Olympians (mostly Zeus) did not make good human beings. The best version of humanity that came before the final generation was undoubtedly the gold generation, as they did not pose any significant threat or challenge to the Titans. Only when the Titans were again involved with the creation of mankind did the blueprint finally stick.

In the ancient world, metals were symbolically attached to divine concepts. The "gold standard" is a really appropriate phrase to apply here, although it might be a bit little cliché. The metals used to describe the different generations of humanity become less and less filled with luster, value, and opulence as time marched on. They also became more rooted to the earth (common metals), but they were more capable of adaptation and preservation and could be directed in a variety of innovative ways. The final generation of humankind, made from clay and water, was the most grounded version. These men were different from the gods, thus making them safe from their divine and vengeful insecurities.

Yet, Zeus still hated them with all his heart. Cooperation was not one of his strong suits, and all of Zeus's wisdom seemed to have left his body the day his daughter Athena was born. When he had discovered that Prometheus had dared raise these humans up to the intellectual and creative level of the gods, he forced Hephaestus to create an "Achilles' heel" for the human race. He created a woman who would unleash unto humanity all the ills of the world.

Pandora, the first woman, was endowed with gifts from all the gods. She was beautiful, cunning, wise, and curious. This perfect specimen of femininity was gifted by Zeus to Epimetheus, who, true to form, cluelessly took Pandora for his wife, not bothering to consider Zeus's intentions. Prometheus smelled a whiff of Zeus's deceit, and he instructed his brother not to accept a wedding gift from the king of the gods. On the day of Pandora's wedding, Zeus handed her a large jar and instructed the couple to never try and open the vessel for a great power dwelled within that could escape through even the smallest crack.

Prometheus begged his brother and sister-in-law to return the gift, but they refused, not wanting to offend the great Zeus. Over time, the temptation grew too much, and Pandora could no longer resist not knowing what was in the jar. She lifted the top ever so slightly, and in the same instant, a thousand horrors poured forth, hardships that humanity had never known like toil, sickness, all manner of plagues, jealousy, lust, and greed. This was Zeus's plan all along, for humanity to be brought down a peg.

We will always be our own greatest champions and enemies. While human beings are capable of great love and creativity, we also have a natural predilection for self-sabotage.

Chapter Nine – Herakles, the Greatest Hero of Them All

He was known as Hercules to the Romans but Herakles (or Heracles) to the Greeks. He was the most highly venerated and favored demi-god amongst the Olympians and mankind. This honor, however, came at a giant cost, for Herakles, without a doubt, has endured more suffering than any other Greek mortal. Even among the immortals and demi-gods of Greek mythology, his strife takes a higher rank.

The story of his chaotic life began the day he was born. He was thrust into a world of family conflict and jealousy. Herakles was the son of Zeus and Alcmene, who was the wife of Amphitryon and the granddaughter of Perseus. Yes, the same Perseus who defeated the Gorgon Medusa; he was also a demi-god sired by Zeus. So, in actuality, Zeus snuck into the bed of his great-great-grand-daughter disguised as her husband and impregnated her with Herakles. When the boy was born, his mother noticed that he showed an incredible degree of strength and physical stamina. This was the only reason he managed to survive his childhood.

Hera, true to form, was none too pleased with her incestuous cheating husband, and honestly, she had plenty of reasons to seek some sort of revenge. One of the saddest arcs of Hera's story as a wife is that she could never punish her husband for his cheating outside of torturing his many mistresses and their children. She loved her husband and didn't want to hurt him. In response to Herakles's birth, Hera sent two large snakes to strangle the infant in his crib. Herakles's strength saved him for the first time. He seized the serpents by their throats and squeezed until their movements ceased.

If Hera could not steal the infant's life, then she would take away his destiny. Before Herakles's birth, Zeus had prophesied that this son would inherit the Mycenean kingdom and become one of the greatest rulers the kingdom had ever seen. Hera managed to place another child as the king of Mycenae, the feeble and premature Eurystheus, the child of Alcmene and Amphitryon. Hera tricked Zeus out of this oath, and thus, Herakles was stripped of his rightful place on the throne.

After Herakles managed to survive Hera's first assassination attempt, the goddess went mad with frustration and decided, as a last resort, to go with one of her usual punishments. She caused the hero to lose his reason and sense of time; ultimately, she drove him mad. She didn't inflict this punishment until years later, when Herakles had reached manhood and was managing to gather some shred of happiness in his life.

After Herakles defeated the Minyans and saved the city of Thebes from being destroyed, he was given the daughter of King Creon, Megara, as a wife. The two were very much in love and had three children together. Although Herakles had found a place of repose, it was ripped away from him in one swift moment of madness. Although he had been able to cope with these fits for years after Hera had first infected his mind, his mental tenacity wore down. One day, he murdered his wife and children. When Herakles came back to his senses, his grief and heartbreak for the loss of not only his life partner but also his beloved children were indescribably unbearable. After some time, he decided to take action. He tracked down Apollo, the god of truth and healing, and he begged his half-brother to either heal him of his grief or strike him down.

Apollo, who knew what his wicked stepmother Hera had done, decided on a different course of action to aid Herakles in his guilt. He told Herakles that it was not his fault what had come to pass and that if he was up to the challenge, there was a way for Herakles to heal and atone for his actions. At the end of this journey, Herakles would attain immortality and no longer suffer from the loss of his wife and children. These actions would come to be known as the twelve labors of Herakles. They were feats of incredible physical and intellectual strength that would come to define and cement this hero's place in mythological history.

Apollo told Herakles to go to his cousin, Eurystheus, who was both his rival and the current king of Mycenae. He had to ask the king to bestow any tasks he could think of upon the demi-god. Herakles must then complete them to regain his honor. Apollo knew he was asking a lot from Herakles in this endeavor, as he would not only go through hell in order to repent but also suffer at the whim of a king whom Herakles considered to be an inferior man. As anyone who has ever worked under an incompetent leader or manager could tell you, this was indeed a challenge.

This Roman relief, dated to the 3rd century CE, depicts the twelve labors of Herakles. From left to right, you can see the Nemean lion, the Lernaean Hydra, the Erymanthian Boar, the Ceryneian Hind, the Stymphalian birds, the girdle of Hippolyta, the Augean stables, the Cretan Bull, and the mares of Diomedes.

(Public Domain,
https://commons.wikimedia.org/wiki/File:Twelve_Labours_Altemps_Inv8642.jpg)

Eurystheus set Herakles twelve impossible tasks, in addition to nine minor tasks (these are often not included in many myths). These tasks had a high risk of death and no real hope for success. However, when dealing with the demi-god of demi-gods, the odds were pretty even. The first of these tasks was defeating the Nemean lion. Perhaps you remember it from before. It was the son of the great terror Typhoeus. The Nemean lion inhabited a cave in the mountain valley of Nemea in the kingdom of Argolis. The lion's hide was impervious to weapons, so in order to defeat this great animal, Herakles would have to go toe to toe with the lion in a contest of strength and will. In classic Greek fashion, Herakles wrested the lion entirely in the nude. (This mirrors the real-world tradition of ancient Olympic wrestling, which was completed entirely in the nude in the dirt, with each wrestler first rubbed down head to toe in oil. Just let that spectacle sit with you.) He managed to grasp the lion around its throat and strangled it to death. Afterward, Herakles skinned the Nemean lion and wore its hide as an impenetrable cloak. He also requested that the figure of his opponent be placed amongst the stars. So, Zeus honored the great lion by casting him as the constellation Leo. This is one of the hero's trademark symbols, and the skin of the great lion aided him in the remainder of his labors.

Next, Herakles traveled to the faraway swamps of Lerna, which was beside the kingdom of Argos. There dwelled the infamous Lernaean Hydra with her nine heads, the middle of which was immortal. This beast was personally reared by Hera, and as such, it was as if the goddess was using her champion against the hero. Hera was no fan of Herakles, after all. This was, without a doubt, the most dangerous foe Herakles had faced to date, and as such, he required the assistance of his good friend Iolaos to best the beast. For this reason, Eurystheus declared the labor unlawfully completed, which meant it would not be counted as a successful quest. Herakles would have to perform and successfully complete an additional labor.

Herakles managed to defeat the Hydra with the aid of Athena and Iolaos. The Hydra also came with its own reinforcements in the form of a giant crab. The goddess instructed Herakles on how to defeat the Hydra. She told him that every time he cut off a head, he would need to cauterize the wound to ensure that another could not grow in its place. So, Herakles fetched an oak branch off a tree nearby and lit it. With his bow and arrow, he shot the Hydra in the torso to subdue it long enough to cut off one head at a time with enough time to brand the wound. After he had repeated the process with each of the heads, there was only the immortal middle head left to defeat. This he crushed with a giant boulder, bringing the Hydra's reign of terror to an end.

After this grueling labor had been completed and denied authorization by the king of Mycenae, Herakles set out on his next task, one that would take nearly a full year to complete. Eurystheus had charged him with capturing the Ceryneian Hind, which is more commonly known as the Golden Stag of Arcadia. This animal was one of five sacred gilded deer gifted to the goddess Artemis by the nymph Taygete, who was one of the more essential and prominent figures of the natural Greek world. She was the daughter of Atlas and Pleione, and she inhabited the mountainous area of Laconia. With Zeus, she would give birth to the ancestors of the king of Sparta. The animals she gifted the goddess were of great importance to Artemis, and all five of them pulled her chariot.

Herakles finally managed to capture the animal by wounding it with an arrow in its flank. At one point, the stag tried to escape its captor, and in the ensuing struggle, Herakles accidentally tore off one of its golden antlers. This was tucked away for safekeeping, and Herakles attempted to haul the animal back to Mycenae on his shoulders. On route to the kingdom, the hero was stopped by Artemis and her brother Apollo. Artemis was furious that her sacred animal had been treated in such a manner, and she sought revenge on Herakles. After hours of arguing back and forth, Herakles managed to calm the goddess's anger, explaining the goal of his twelve labors. The goddess allowed him to haul the animal back to Mycenae just as long as he planned to release the stag after it had been presented to the king. The hard task for this specific labor was not only capturing the animal but also surviving the wrath of a goddess who didn't typically allow such infractions. She would have likely preferred to transform Herakles into a wild animal, one that would be ripped apart by her hunting hounds.

After he had regained his strength, Herakles set out on his next impossible task. This time, he traveled to the snowy mountain region of Erymanthia, where the Erymanthian Boar was known to reside. Occasionally, the great beast would come down from the mountains to hunt and terrorize the villages of mortal men in the farmlands of Psophis. So, Herakles traveled all the way up the snowy mountain to a cave where the boar was resting. The boar caught the scent of our hero and charged him as he was standing at the entrance of the cave. Herakles jumped swiftly out of the way, and the chase was on. He ran after the boar for a good couple of hours, finally netting the great beast. He managed to take the boar alive all the way to the chamber of Eurystheus.

Upon seeing the terror that was the great Erymanthian Boar, Eurystheus, true to his cowardly nature, dove headfirst into a giant pithos jar that was buried underneath the earth. Herakles took the opportunity to tease his cousin and acted like he would shove the live boar into the jar with the king, which caused Eurystheus to cower even further inside the vessel. This gained a chuckle from the rest of the people in the throne room. When the king finally emerged from his hiding place, he gave Herakles his next labor and made sure this one would pay the hero back for his torturous behavior.

Herakles was charged with cleaning the stables of King Augeas, who ruled over the Epeians of Elis in the western region of the Peloponnese. This was not the noblest of tasks, and the job needed to be completed in one day, which was practically impossible, considering that there was about a week's worth of oxen feces caked to the floor of the barn. True to form, Herakles gave the same dedication to the labor as the other ones for the right price. Some say he was to be paid in gold, while some sources indicate that Herakles had been promised a quarter of the oxen. The king was sure he would never have to reward Herakles because there was no earthly way that he could perform the task in one day. The king promised to pay the hero a fair wage for his assistance, and the two men shook on their deal.

With his great strength, Herakles managed to push giant boulders into the River Alpheus, diverting the stream onto the plain and into the barn. The strength of the water washed away the manure from all twenty oxen and swept away the dirt and impurities from the stalls. King Augeas couldn't believe the ease with which the hero completed the task and refused to pay Herakles what he was due. The hero was so angered that he swore destruction on the entire kingdom of Elis. When his labors were completed, he would come back and exact his terrible vengeance on the land and its people. His campaign was delayed for quite some time after the completion of this labor due to a lack of resources and an army, as well as a sudden illness that befell the hero. However, when Herakles regained his strength, he overtook Elis just as he had promised and crushed the skull of the king with his bare hands.

Before all that transpired, though, Herakles needed to continue with his labors for the good of his soul. The sixth labor was to rid the world of the Stymphalian birds that lived on Lake Stymphalia in Arcadia. These man-eating birds were initially discovered by Jason and the Argonauts, who found out the hard way their proclivity for the flesh of anything and everything. After that, these birds developed a taste for man meat and became the terror of Arcadia. In addition to their hardy appetite, the birds could also shoot razor-sharp feathers from their wings that sliced through the air like arrows. The parentage of the birds is hotly debated, but one thing the ancient scholars all agreed upon is that these birds were raised for some period of time by the god of war, Ares. As such, the god probably used the giant raptors in one or all of his many battles, although they are never named directly.

Herakles was not fazed one bit by what were surely some terrifying birds. He drew them out from their hiding places in the thick bushes and vines that ran along the eastern side of the lake by creating loud noises by casting large stones against one another. As each bird flew to attack him, he shot them out of the sky with his arrows. Now you may ask yourself, how come no one ever succeeded in killing the birds this way before? The propulsion of Herakles's arrows and the swing of his sword were mightier than most men. When he shot an arrow from his bow, the strength was almost akin to the shot from Zeus's lightning bolt. Herakles's strength made him closer to the gods than humans.

The seventh labor of Herakles features perhaps one of the most famous mythical animals in Greek legends: the Cretan Bull. This bull fathered the Minotaur with the queen of Crete, who had seen the beauty of the animal and couldn't help but be overcome by unimaginable lust. Bestiality was not common in ancient Greece, so this act would have been very disturbing to the average Greek.

The Cretan Bull was said to be born of the sea as a gift to mankind by the god Poseidon, and it was to be sacrificed in his honor. However, when the king of Crete saw the beauty of the animal, he could not offer it in sacrifice. Instead, he turned the bull out to pasture and gave another in homage to the god of the sea. Naturally, this was not a good idea, and Poseidon cursed the king, saying that the bull would be the ruin of him. He drove the creature mad to the point where it pursued the queen (who herself had been driven mad with longing for the bull, most likely by Poseidon as an act of revenge) and continuously terrorized the people.

Herakles now needed to capture the animal and take it all the way back to Mycenae to present to the king. He succeeded in his task and afterward set the creature free to return to its home island. Why he freed the bull and the boar after killing many of the other animals and creatures involved in his labors cannot be said. However, it would seem that the Cretan Bull was a god in its own right; it was certainly on the same divine level as Herakles since it was a child of one of the big three gods—the brothers Zeus, Poseidon, and Hades. Perhaps Herakles respected the bull far too much to put an end to his life. It was not until the hero Theseus that the days of the Cretan Bull came to an end, and his likeness was placed among the constellations as the astrological symbol Taurus.

Herakles's eighth labor was the most devastating to his soul. After he had released the Cretan Bull, Eurystheus issued a more dangerous task for Herakles to complete, something that would test his constitution as a demi-god. Herakles had faced off against many evil creatures during his labors, even creatures that hungered for human flesh, but such was their way as natural predators. In his eighth labor, Herakles would encounter something far more sinister: a human being who fed the flesh of other human beings to his animals.

The king of Thrace, the terrible son of Ares and Cyrene, was Diomedes. He fed his horse a diet of human flesh, which turned the poor animals away from their natural gentle inclinations, turning them into beasts unrecognizable as horses with unnatural aggression. In the dead of night, Herakles, with a few very brave volunteers, set off to kill the guards to the king's stables, after which he captured the horses and placed them on a ship that was waiting at the coast. With the animals successfully captured, Herakles dismissed the volunteers to sail back home, leaving the horses under the charge of his squire and long-time friend Abderus, a son of Hermes.

While Herakles was in pursuit of Diomedes, Abderus was attacked and eaten by the mares. Diomedes had done his work well; the horses were uncontrollable, even for a demi-god and experienced warrior like Abderus. After Diomedes had been captured, Herakles returned to the ship, where he discovered the remains that were once his best friend. In anger, he found the king and fed him alive to his horses. This seemed to quell the horses' insatiable appetite for man flesh. Herakles hauled the steeds back to Mycenae and presented them to the king, who once again scoffed at Herakles's efforts. Our hero was too devastated over the loss of Abderus to respond.

At this point, Herakles was tired of fighting. For the ninth labor, he sought every sort of road possible to peacefully achieve his quest. Eurystheus next asked him to bring him the belt of Hippolyta. She was the queen of the Amazons and one of the greatest warriors in Greece. She certainly had the most feared cavalry. Amazon warriors were known for charging into battle on horses and mowing their opponents down. These were no ordinary warriors Herakles was up against, and if possible, he wanted to avoid a fight.

When he arrived on the shores of the Amazons' island with his company of warriors (just in case), Hippolyta came down to the beach with her entourage of fighters. She inquired why one of the most legendary heroes in all of Greece had rowed all the way to her shores. Herakles informed her of his request. He knew the weight of what he was asking of Queen Hippolyta. The belt had been gifted to her by Ares, and as such, it was irreplaceable.

Surprisingly, Hippolyta was more than willing to hand over the belt in order for Herakles to complete his tasks. It is unknown why the queen showed such selfless generosity, but perhaps she had heard tell of the hero's labors and pitied him for having to suffer such an ordeal. Hera, however, suspected ill of Herakles and his company and decided to start a fight, just to be safe. She proceeded to go from Amazon to Amazon, whispering to their inner conscience that Herakles was there to kidnap the queen. The Amazons, having all had this same collective thought, suited up for battle, mounted their horses, and charged down to the beach. Seeing the entire army coming his way, Herakles ordered his men to slay the queen's warriors. He shoved his sword into the queen's chest and ripped the belt from her body. He made a quick getaway before the army reached the shore, making off with a belt that he had sought to acquire peacefully but did so in blood due to another goddess's insecurities. He took the blood-stained belt back to Eurystheus and laid it before the king's feet. Eurystheus then gave Herakles his next task.

On the island of Erytheia in the westernmost known reaches of the earth, somewhere near Iberia, lived a giant who went by the name of Geryon. He was a peaceful enough giant, despite his very intimidating presence. He was known for his three torsos and four sets of wings. He was the son of two great forces of nature, Callirhoe and Chrysaor. His mother, Callirhoe, was a rain nymph from his native Erytheia, and his father, Chrysaor, was a giant, the son of Medusa and the twin brother of Pegasus. Geryon was definitely one of the strongest contenders that our hero had come up against thus far.

The task was to bring King Eurystheus the peaceful giant's prized herd of cattle, the red calves of Geryon. The light of the magnificent sunset that fell over the western waters had stained the entire herd red. It is no coincidence that the "red calf" trope appears in one of Greek mythology's most well-known stories, as it is seen in many ancient sources. The Greeks indeed got around and were more than willing to share their stories with other societies and vice versa. Some of the most influential literature in history has come out of the Mediterranean region.

So off Herakles went on his task, borrowing his mode of transportation from Helios. The sun was kind enough to lend Herakles his solid gold drinking vessel, which was large enough to row across the sea to the island of Erytheia. Of course, the physics of this transportation is iffy at best, but one has to imagine there was a great deal of rowing on Herakles's part. Regardless, he sailed the seas in a giant cup.

In order to acquire the cattle, Herakles would need to fight his way past the two levels of security that Geryon had set up to look after his beloved herd. Herakles's first task would be to get past the shepherd, the fearsome giant Eurytion, then somehow best the fearsome two-headed canine Orthros. And then after that, if he was still in one piece, he would need to go toe to toe with the three-bodied Geryon himself. One has to think that Herakles would have rather gone after one hundred Nemean lions rather than attempt to steal any cattle from Geryon. But penance is penance, and Herakles had to endure this punishment to relieve his suffering from murdering his family. Of course, one has to wonder at what point had Herakles suffered enough.

Herakles managed to slay the cattle herder and then the brave Orthros. Finally, he found himself facing the terrible Geryon, who stood stoic, ready to protect what was his. In terms of the law,

Herakles had come to kill and steal, although he is meant to be seen as the protagonist of this tale. However, if one looks at it from the other angle, he is also the antagonist. In the end, Herakles drove his sword into the back of Geryon and then herded the cattle on board his ship and set sail back to the Peloponnese.

Thus far, Herakles had successfully completed ten of the twelve tasks assigned to him. There were two more. Eurystheus tasked Herakles with retrieving the golden apples from Hera's tree and bringing them back to Mycenae so that a tree might be planted in the king's garden. The tree and its fruit were guarded by the Hesperides, the daughters of Nyx. They were the goddesses of the golden light of dusk. They were named Aegle, Erytheia, Hesperidia, and Arethusa.

These goddesses guarded the precious treasures of not only Queen Hera but also all the immortals. When Perseus set out on his quest to slay the Gorgon Medusa, he also stopped to visit the Hesperides in order to obtain weapons powerful enough to slay a Gorgon. Despite the Hesperides being charged with the protection of these items, they were not always the perfect security detail. One assumes that their parentage afforded them such a position of power.

Together, these four women stood guard over Hera's tree. It was a precious gift given to her by Gaia on the day of her wedding to Zeus. The Hesperides were also assisted in their watch by a hundred-headed serpent who went by the name of Ladon. Herakles had already bested more fearsome monsters than a hundred-headed dragon, and as such, this task was probably a walk in the park for our hero. He easily delayed the dragon and then proceeded to take the apples by force, once again ferrying them all the way back to Mycenae to be left in the hands of an ungrateful king.

Atlas, the Titan condemned to hold up the sky, plays an interesting role in the more popular version of this myth. On his way to gather the apples, Herakles found Atlas. Since it was his daughters who oversaw the apples, he thought Atlas would have an easier time. Someone had to hold the world up, though, and Herakles took the burden upon his shoulders so his task could be fulfilled. Atlas retrieved the apples as requested and was then kind enough to offer to deliver them to the king himself.

But Herakles was not moved by the Titan's compassion. He suspected that if Atlas left with the apples, he would never return. Instead of playing his hand, Herakles agreed but asked if Atlas could take the world for a moment so he could make himself more comfortable. Atlas sat the apples down and shouldered his burden once more. Herakles did not hesitate; he grabbed the apples and ran.

In a variation of the myth, Athena righted this wrong before the precious fruit could be carved open and their seeds extracted. She stole the apples from the king's personal chambers and returned them to the Hesperides. Most versions end with Herakles successfully delivering the apples, though.

The final task that King Eurystheus set for our hero was to retrieve the three-headed guard dog of the underworld and the pride of the great Hades: Cerberus. This task was probably one of the most treacherous in terms of location, given the fact that many heroes had succeeded in entering the underworld, but few were victorious in actually leaving in one piece or at all. Herakles managed to capture the hound with the help of Hermes, Athena, and Persephone. Given the sheer number of immortals needed to execute this plan successfully indicates the mess Herakles would have been in if he had attempted the task on his own. Hermes lent Herakles his winged shoes in order for him to gain more speed. Athena revealed the best ways to tackle the beast by using the dog's weight against him. Finally, Persephone would aid Herakles in getting back to the surface with his prize.

After this, Herakles's labors had been completed, and his guilt had been absolved for the crime of murdering his wife and three children. At the end of the labors, the gods were impressed with Herakles's physical and mental tenacity and awarded him a seat on Olympus, along with immortality.

Chapter Ten – Jason and the Argonauts

Greek myths involving the most famous heroes, be they demi-gods or full human beings, always start with some sort of dramatic backstory, a tale to build up the coming drama of the hero's journey. Just like in the real world, our stories do not start with us; they start with stories that come before us, building into a collective narrative of interconnected lives. The legendary myth of Jason and the Argonauts has been reflected and drawn from in various adaptations. People are still retelling the morals of this amazing tale and basing new stories on names and concepts used in the original myth thousands of years after the story was first told.

The story of Jason and the Argonauts begins with a golden fleece that belonged to a winged ram. No one knows the origin of this particular ram. All that is known is the unfortunate fate of the animal and the destiny it provided one Greek hero. The ram was captured by King Aeetes of Colchis and sacrificed to the gods. However, the ram's golden fleece was preserved from the sacrificial flames and locked away from the daylight and the eyes of other mortal kings who would seek to possess the fleece's inherent wealth and magical power. The king hid the fleece in a far-off cave on the island of Colchis and employed the services of a fire-breathing dragon to guard the fleece day and night. If you have ever read Tolkien, you now know where the dragon-like characteristic of guardians and hoarding treasure originates, for this theme was employed in the myth of Jason and the Argonauts.

Centuries later, on the island of Iolkos (Iolcus) in Thessaly, the good King Aeson gave birth to his son and heir, Jason. Like all good family dramas in the ancient world, sibling bonds counted for very little. King Aeson's half-brother Pelias sought to take control of his brother's throne. He accomplished this easily enough by poisoning the reigning king. Jason's mother, Queen Alcimede, was not so easily fooled as the rest of her husband's court. It is also possible they themselves had been privy to the heinous murder of her beloved husband. To keep her son safe from the clutches of her brother-in-law, Alcimede sent Jason away to be raised by the centaur Cheiron (also spelled as Chiron). Shortly after she turned her son over to Cheiron, Alcimede died, succumbing to heartbreak over the death of her husband and the separation from her only son, whom she was sure she would never see again.

Jason's new guardian, Cheiron, was the wisest and the oldest of his kind. The centaurs were a breed and tribal confederation of half-horse men that inhabited Thessaly. Cheiron was, in fact, the half-brother of Zeus, and as such, he was a very respected figure in the Greek world for his prowess as a capable leader. He was also known for his intellect and kindness. Cheiron nurtured the young Jason, teaching him invaluable life skills, such as reading and writing in several languages, self-defense, and offensive fighting tactics. Cheiron was the living embodiment of strength through grace, and his name is seen in many different Greek myths. He is heralded as potentially the most famous centaur in Greek mythology. If anyone reading this has ever read any Percy Jackson books, the figure of Cheiron appears there; he is the trainer of all the demi-gods in the modern world.

When Jason grew into a man, he asked Cheiron to let him go before the king and demand his rightful inheritance to the throne. Cheiron was very fond of his protégé and ward. He did not want to see the boy he had raised go before a mad and dishonest king. But Cheiron knew that this was Jason's destiny, and as such, he told him to go before the king but keep his wits about him. Jason knew that he would never be able to slay his uncle in the throne room with so many swords pointed at his back. He would come in a diplomatic fashion and demand the return of his throne.

Years before, Jason's uncle, King Pelias, still fearing for the security of his throne, visited the Oracle of Delphi and consulted her as to what his fate might be if Jason should return. Pelias had no guarantee that his nephew was indeed dead, for he had no knowledge of what Alcimede did. He certainly would never have guessed that Jason would be left under the charge of one of the most feared and respected creatures of the ancient world. The Oracle informed Pelias to be wary of a man that came before him without one of his sandals.

Hera, who had overheard everything Pelias confessed that day, sought to end the evil king and his lordship over Iolkos. Years prior, Pelias had murdered his stepmother in cold blood at the entrance to Hera's temple. For fear that someone would discover what he had done, especially the goddess, he banned all his subjects from worshiping at the temple of Hera. Hera was one of the more insecure goddesses who needed lots of attention, and if she didn't get it, she could be ruthless. She was definitely the wrong divine being to mess with because if anyone mortal or immortal knew how to hang onto a grudge, it was Hera. She was always seeking out chances for revenge, and this time, she would make sure that Pelias suffered for his crimes against her and her worshipers.

On Jason's way back to the palace, he saw an old woman trying to cross a treacherous river. He assisted her, but he lost one of his sandals in the current. Pelias would have liked to chop Jason's head off right then and there when he saw the young man enter his throne room with one sandal, but he knew that this would tarnish his reputation as king and potentially shine a light on his brother's untimely and somewhat suspicious death. All rulers find it exceptionally hard to rule a kingdom that despises their very existence. At some level, kings and queens do need to care about how their people consider them as rulers.

However, Pelias was very cunning. He, too, sought to deal with the issue in a diplomatic fashion. He informed Jason that he would return the throne to him if he retrieved the coveted golden fleece from the dragon-guarded cave on the island of Colchis. He believed that his nephew would never be able to beat the beast and that he would more than likely die on the quest.

However, Jason would not be going alone. He commissioned one of the best shipwrights in all of Greece, Argos, to build him the largest and sturdiest ship the Greek world had ever seen. Under the guidance of the patron goddess of craft Athena, Argos built the *Argo*, a twenty-two-meter-long vessel with fifty oars and a low drought that allowed the ship to take on a considerable amount of water without foundering. The oars, anchor, and mast were all removable, which allowed the vessel to be rolled onto the shore of any landmass. This would prevent the ship from being destroyed in their absence or stolen.

Crafted from the oak and pine trees of Iolkos, the *Argo* was a blessed vessel, and the men aboard her sturdy deck were nothing but the finest soldiers in all of Greek mythology. These men were known as the Argonauts. The word Argonauts is translated from ancient Greek as "Argo sailors," with "nauts" meaning sailor or voyager. Some of the most famous heroes of Greece came to aid Jason in his quest, including the demi-god Herakles. The Argonauts numbered around fifty men and demi-gods, who were all willing to fight or die trying for the glory of the rightful king of Iolkos. Although they knew they were taking part in 'a noble deed and serving the rightful king, the men also wanted their names to be remembered. Being involved in such a dangerous quest would surely get their names written down in the book of Greek history, whether or not they survived the experience.

Jason and his crew first docked on the island of Lemnos in order to find fresh water and possibly resupply their food stores. When they landed on the shores of Lemnos, they noticed a distinct foul odor in the air. The island reeked of dead fish. They scoured up and down the shores, looking for whatever marine life carcass was causing such a horrific smell. Little did they know that the smell was coming from the inhabitants of Lemnos. Years prior to the arrival of Jason and his soldiers, the island of Lemnos was once a place of peace and prosperity. That is up until the moment its inhabitants neglected to regularly worship the goddess Aphrodite. It is a symbolic irony that even gods and goddesses, in all their seeming perfection, were often the most insecure. This is something that is true of most humans as well.

Despite her legendary beauty and seemingly confident persona, Aphrodite was rife with insecurities. She often wondered if she deserved her place on Olympus, and despite being the patron goddess of one of the most sought-after human experiences in the world (love and sex), she was less loved by the people of Greece. No one seemed to worship or respect her on the same level as some of the other goddesses, like Athena. Women and men alike respected, admired, and prayed often to that goddess. One of the most famous cities in the ancient world and by far the most famous in all of Greece, Athens, was named after Athena.

So, when the lovely ladies of Lemnos dropped the ball on offering regular prayers and sacrifices to Aphrodite, that did not go over well. Perhaps the women of Lemnos were too busy with their daily lives to make it to every temple and shrine, or maybe they did this as a deliberate insult to the goddess. Either way, it did not end well for the women or their husbands. Aphrodite cursed all the women of the island to reek of a foul fish odor, and she made sure there was no cure. And the smell was foul. It greatly affected the lives of the Lemnos women but none more so than their sex lives. Husbands turned away from their wives, and the young ladies yearning to get married were not attracting any suitors. The men of Lemnos were probably 10 percent faster on foot than every other man of Greece because they were constantly running away from the women of their island.

Eventually, all of the husbands took to bedding their Thracian slave girls, who were not affected by the curse. Angry and heartbroken, the women of Lemnos proceeded to murder every man on the island, even the younger boys. They could no longer deal with the rejection and humiliation that came with their affliction. This was the true intention of Aphrodite's curse: first loneliness and then utter extinction. However, the Lemnos ladies moved on and functioned as any Greek society might. They elected a queen to rule over them, Queen Hypsipyle.

After a while, the women accepted the fact that they would never know romantic love or affection again—well, heterosexually anyway. Still, they did have a serious population problem. And although the women suffered, they wanted to continue the culture and polity of their island. But to do that, they needed children. They were out of luck there. All the men were buried or gone, and they couldn't just steal men from the other cities and islands of Greece. That was an easy way to start a war they could not possibly win.

Their luck changed when Jason and the Argonauts arrived on the shores of Lemnos. These sailors were more than ready to fall into the arms of any woman who crossed their path. Now, you may ask yourself, how in the world did the Argonauts and Jason stand the fish smell wafting off these women? Well, when Aphrodite saw that her curse had been fulfilled, she gave the women a break and changed the conditions so that the women would reek of dead fish only on certain days of the year. Over time, the women also learned how to manage the condition with native root plants that grew on the island so that they were not as rancid when those days of the year finally came around.

This seemed to have worked well enough because after six years, the island was back to its original population size. Queen Hypsipyle took Jason as her personal companion, and she was his first lover. Together, they conceived twin boys, Thous and Euneus. After those six years, Jason worried that his men were becoming too comfortable in the beds of these women and that in another year, they would not want to leave their new families. So, he ordered his men to prepare for their journey, and in the morning, while their lovers and wives slept, they set sail once more into the horizon.

They traveled on the sea from Lemnos to the Hellespont and the Propontis (Sea of Marmara), now located in modern-day Turkey. Lemnos was a Greek island located in the northern Aegean, so while the trip was not that lengthy, the men still needed to freshen up their water supply on this particular leg of the voyage. The land of the Propontis was ruled over by King Cyzicus. The king's generosity toward his people was legendary, and he was extremely welcoming of strangers, treating them as honored guests under his own roof.

King Cyzicus greeted Jason and his men with open arms and decided to host a fine and expensive banquet for the Argonauts and toast to the good fortune of their journey. What a time they must have had because the king's men and the Argonauts passed out right in the banquet hall. The next morning, the Argonauts woke up before the king, who was sleeping off a fairly nasty hangover. They went out into the wild to collect supplies for the remainder of their journey. In all of the merriment and drinking, the king kept forgetting to warn Jason of the terrible creatures that plagued his otherwise perfect kingdom.

The Argonauts sailed to another portion of the Hellespont and left Herakles in charge of the ship while they searched for game and water. As Herakles was lying on the sand with the sun in his face, he heard a rumble from deep within the earth. As it grew, the ground started to vibrate with intensity. Herakles jumped to his feet and ran back for the ship as the huge Gegenees burst through the layers of the earth. The Gegenees were giants with six arms. Herakles feared that without his men, he would be beaten by the Gegenees.

They were going to try and attack the ship so that the Argonauts could not escape. Brave Herakles managed to hold them off for an impressive amount of time, all the while yelling and screaming for reinforcements. Jason was the first to hear the cry of his comrade and commanded the Argonauts to return to the ship, their swords drawn. They got down to the beach and stood aghast at the site of the Gegenees. After many relentless hours of fighting the giants, the Argonauts were victorious and hopped back onto the *Argo* before any more misfortune could come their way. However, they had no way of knowing that the greatest tragedy of the journey was yet to come.

By the time Jason and his men were able to set sail, it was well past sundown, and sailing on the seas at night was difficult, given the fact that any light was swallowed by the dark abyss around the ship. The Argonauts meant to sail away from the Propontis, but in the confusion of the night, they sailed right back toward the land of the Doliones, the inhabitants of the Hellespont. Good King Cyzicus saw a ship approaching his coast from his balcony in the throne room, but he could not make out the ship's inhabitants. All he saw was the light of their few torches. Since the king was not expecting any more visitors, he thought that Jason and his men were pirates who had come to lay waste to his shores. The king ordered his men down to the docks and told them to be armed and prepared for battle. The Argonauts were unaware that the king and his army were going to lead an attack against them. All they heard were the war horns of someone, and thinking they were far away from the land of

Propontis, they did not deduce that it was, in fact, their friend and ally sending the charge to attack them.

Amidst all the confusion, King Cyzicus was slain by a rogue arrow, and he died right there on the deck of his ship. When light broke the horizon, both the Argonauts and Cyzicus's men were horrified. They despaired over the death of one of the finest rulers the kingdoms had ever seen. They held a grand funeral for the legendary Cyzicus, and every person in the kingdom, from the city to the countryside, came to honor his memory. The crowd was sobbing for a life that had been so needlessly lost, but none more so than our hero Jason, for he felt responsible for the death of his friend and ally. Although everyone assured Jason that Cyzicus's death was an accident, one that was provoked by the king himself, Jason carried that sunken feeling of absolute guilt for the remainder of his days.

As if the death of Cyzicus was not enough, the Argonauts had not seen the end of death, misery, and loss. Off the coast of Mysia, the *Argo* nearly crashed onto a body of rock formations. In order to divert the ship in time, Herakles dug his oar into the waves and managed to steer the ship out of danger. However, just as the ship cleared the rocks, Herakles's oar snapped right in two. He told Jason that he intended to go ashore with Hylas, his beloved squire, in order to find another large oak tree, from which he would fashion a new oar. Jason agreed, and off the two men went into the forest.

While Herakles went on his search for the perfect oak tree, Hylas, ever the loyal and loving ward, went to fetch fresh water for his master so that he would have something to quench his thirst while he worked on the oar. Hylas found a cool mountain lake, clear as crystal, with waters that seemed to glimmer, gleam, and even flirt with the young man as he approached. Little did Hylas know that the waters were indeed flirting with him. This was the work of a water nymph. She emerged onto the smooth rock shore of the lake and lured Hylas into the water with sweet words and kisses that lapped at his feet. Eventually, Hylas followed her so far into the water that his head went under the smooth waves. Since he was bewitched by the immortal nymph's spell of love, Hylas was unaware that he had begun to drown.

After some time, Herakles noticed that his friend had failed to return. Hylas never left his master's side for this amount of time. Herakles called out for him and searched far and wide, but his squire failed to answer. Herakles began to become hysterical, and he ran down to the *Argo* to request a search party. Most of the Argonauts did not see the need for such a fuss over one squire, but Herakles refused to leave without Hylas. This began to break down the relations on the *Argo*, with half the men refusing to leave without Herakles and the other unwilling to postpone the progression of the journey. Soon, Jason faced the threat of a mutiny.

However, Hera (remember, she had a lot staked on the success of Jason and his men) sent word to the sea god Glaucus, the patron god of fishermen. He was the ideal being to pacify and mediate the situation, given the fact that Glaucus had once been human; he had gained immortality by eating a very rare sea herb that had been sewn into creation by Cronos himself. Glaucus knew very well the tensions that could be aboard a vessel and reassured the Argonauts that it was the will of the gods that Herakles stay on land to search for his friend.

Before they set sail once more into the breach, Glaucus advised Jason to leave Herakles a second-in-command, so Jason ordered Polyphemus to stay behind with Greece's greatest hero and make sure he came to no harm. If Herakles perished, it would be Polyphemus's responsibility to make his way back in order to report the death.

Now missing two of their most skilled warriors, the Argonauts set sail with a pit in their stomachs. Even though Glaucus had reassured them that this was fated, they still felt less than confident about surviving the remainder of their journey, especially since they were sailing toward their next destination to restock their stores. In northwestern Anatolia was the land of King Amycus (or Amykos), lord of the Bebryces, a hoard of stocky bare-knuckle fighters that were feared throughout mainland Greece, Asia Minor, and Mycenae.

Amycus was actually a demi-god himself. He was the son of Melia, the naiad daughter of the Titan Oceanus, and Poseidon. Given his parentage, Amycus had inherited both his mother's and father's turbulent nature and sought to fight any stranger who dared step foot on his lands. Seeing Jason and the Argonauts roll onto his shores greatly angered and intrigued the king, as word had already spread throughout Asia Minor of Jason and the Argonauts and their quest for the golden fleece.

King Amycus approached the Argonauts and challenged Jason to a fistfight right there on the spot. One of Jason's better qualities as a man and a leader was recognizing where his strengths lay, and he knew that he was no match for a demi-god son of Poseidon. In the most gracious manner, he beseeched Amycus that he might be able to select one of his men to fight in his stead, for who would be responsible for the well-being and command of the Argonauts if he should fall. Jason made it seem like his chosen tribute would have no chance of winning the fight against Amycus, and so, the king of the Bebryces accepted Jason's offer. Little did Amycus know that in Jason's company was the legendary boxer Polydeuces, who was also a son of Zeus.

The fight was well-matched, demi-god against demi-god, and what a fight it was. There were plenty of nail-biting moments where it seemed that either boxer could be the victor. Right hooks landed firmly on jawlines, and the spectators witnessed fast dodges and swings that would have taken the head off of most mortals. However, in the end, Polydeuces had bested Amycus. He managed to kill the king with an uppercut right to Amycus's lower jaw. The sheer amount of force broke the king's jaw and shoved his nose bone into the fore of his brain. The scene was grotesque, to say the least, and Amycus died a horrible death.

The Bebryces were outraged over the inhumane death of their king and sought to avenge his death by doing away with Jason and the Argonauts. They were no match for Jason's cunning wit and intellect, though. Jason had undoubtedly realized that Polydeuces was the superior fighter when he set the challenge, and he had already prepared for the outcome of what would happen if Amycus fell. As the fight between the two men was drawing to its close, Jason had his men slowly move into their main fighting formation so that when the Bebryces attacked, they would be ready. The Argonauts managed to push back the attack and drove their enemies into the hills.

After reboarding the *Argo*, the men sailed past the Bosporus (or Bosphorus, a strait in northwestern Turkey) and finally made port in the land of Thrace. After trudging for some time on foot, searching for more supplies, they came upon a man who was just sitting down to enjoy his midday meal. Jason went to approach the man to ask him where they might find game to hunt when all of a sudden, two winged and beastly creatures appeared from seemingly nowhere and began to torment the man. At first, Jason ordered his men not to engage these creatures, but when he saw that the man was blind and that the beasts were desecrating his food, he and the Argonauts engaged them and drove them away. They helped the man reset his camp, light his fire, and get him a fresh pot of food back on the flame. The man was so grateful to the Argonauts that he invited them to join him for the meal and revealed himself to be Phineas, a legendary seer who had been gifted with visions of the future. Phineas could predict all potential variables for changes in the destiny of men and all potential outcomes of the future.

His greatest gift also became his curse. Phineas lost his eyesight because of his predictions concerning the many offspring of Zeus.

The lord of the skies did not need his already crazed and jealous queen knowing the whereabouts of his potential wives and children. Phineas was able to expose Zeus to any common stranger. Phineas would discuss the fate of men very casually, and he knew the information could circulate its way back to Hera through her network of prayers and spies. Also, she was a goddess and very tuned in to the world of women.

Zeus cursed Phineas, causing him to go blind all of a sudden. He could have easily killed the seer, but in the end, Phineas was a useful and rare source of information, only secondary to the Oracle of Delphi. Zeus's curse was a warning shot, alerting Phineas that he was to keep his mouth shut from now on. However, Zeus had plenty of petty nature in his godly form and wanted to make sure Phineas wouldn't suddenly have a wave of courage and go back to his old ways. So, Zeus sent the Harpies to visit Phineas every once in a while. They tormented and intimidated the old man, reminding him who was in charge. This torture was too much to bear, and it traumatized Phineas to the point where he no longer attempted to see the future. He was too afraid to even use his gift.

So, the Argonauts and Phineas talked through the night, with the young sailors, heroes, and demi-gods all enthralled by the stories and knowledge of the old seer. This was the most Phineas had spoken to other people in years, and he spoke freely. He then heard the story of the Argonauts' journey, the lands they had visited, their tragedies, and their triumphs. Phineas was so moved and compelled by their journey that he offered them his services; he would look into their future and predict their best outcome for survival. However, in return for his visionary guidance, he requested that the Argonauts help him dispense of his tormentors, the vicious Harpies. Jason and his men were already quite fond of Phineas, and they agreed to help.

Luckily for the Argonauts, this was not a big favor to ask, as they were well equipped to deal with the situation. Two in Jason's crew,

Zetes and Calais, were the children of Boreas, the Titan of the north wind. They were very capable flyers. The Harpies didn't stand much of a chance in the grand scheme of things since they were far less agile flyers. If it had not been for their sister Iris, who intervened at the last second, the Harpies would have been slaughtered. (Yes, the same Iris who was the goddess of the rainbow and the messenger of the gods.) Iris made the Argonauts a promise that the Harpies would leave the old man be. She also said that Zeus would not be made aware of their absence so long as Phineas thought twice about whose future he looked into.

After Iris and the Harpies departed, Phineas looked into the future of the Argonauts' journey and saw the Symplegades or Clashing Rocks. These were two giant boulders that had once been a whole island. This island was split from the seafloor by Poseidon. The boulders had a tendency to shift apart and then crash back together again, but for a few perilous minutes, the passageway would be open. This was the fastest way to the other side. It was the route that the Argonauts would have to brave if they wanted to stay the course and not add a lot of additional time to their journey. Time was always on Jason's mind; the crew had lost so much time at the beginning of their journey that they could not afford to waste more. Phineas told them they could time their sail through the Symplegades by sending a white dove through first. If she made the journey and returned, they would know it was safe enough to sail through.

When the Argonauts approached the massive rocks, they were unlike anything one could imagine. And the passageway between them was even more narrow than Phineas had originally described. The worst part, of course, was the small amount of time the rocks seemed to stay apart from one another. It seemed to truly be a matter of minutes before the two boulders crashed together again. If the ship attempted to sail between them, it was obvious the men and the *Argo* would be wiped clean from the face of the earth forever, with not even their bones remaining intact.

Jason was willing to take the risk. He believed that it was worth it, and this gave his men courage. They sailed as close as they could without being pulled into the current of the rocks, and then they sent out the dove. She was gone for a little while but returned to the ship safe and seemingly unharmed. The Argonauts took this as a blessing and decided to attempt the pass. They prayed to the gods for strength and speed and set their oars.

Onward they rowed, entering the passageway with fear in their hearts but strength in their conviction. They could hear the sounds of the rocks creaking and moaning in the seas, sounds coming from the lowest depths of the earth, the sound of rushing anxious water sloshing back and forth against every inch of the ship. It was not smooth sailing by any means. What's worse was the disappearing light. Jason began to notice that the sun's rays were growing weaker and weaker, a sign that the tops of the boulders would crash together at any minute. Jason ordered his men to row for their lives as he steered the ship through the perilous pathway. The light was dying, the tunnel was becoming increasingly dark as they rowed on, and Jason feared they would not make it through after all.

Just then, it was as if the boulders ceased to be moving toward one another. They miraculously had just stopped moving altogether. Jason could not see Athena, but she was at the top, holding the two boulders apart, which gave the Argonauts just enough time to make it through. As soon as they were clear, she let the two cliffs meet once more.

The remainder of the Argonauts' journey to Colchis was relatively uneventful other than a surprise attack by the remainder of the Stymphalian birds, those birds that managed to survive Herakles a few years prior. Herakles's defeat of the birds had echoed throughout Greece, and pretty much every person had a basic concept of how to drive the beasts away with loud noises.

Jason and his men went to work throwing objects at the birds and beating their swords and spears against their shields, fending the birds off as they did so. They managed to succeed but lost one of their crew, Oileus, in the ensuing frenzy. He was struck in the chest by one of the razor-sharp feathers and was dead before he hit the deck of the *Argo*.

Finally, Jason and his men had completed their voyage and arrived on the island of Colchis. Hera had been in their company for the entire journey and had planned from the outset to aid Jason in his ultimate quest of obtaining the golden fleece from the clutches of a dragon, if not purely for her own gain. No matter how brave Jason was, he was only a man. He was not impervious to flame and fire, and he was completely devoid of any physically superior gifts like those that had been bestowed on Herakles. As they approached Colchis, Jason wished more than ever that he had convinced Herakles to remain aboard the *Argo*.

However, he was unaware of the plan that the goddess Hera had concocted in order for him to survive. King Aeetes happened to have a daughter, Medea, the high priestess of Hecate, who was the goddess of magic. And it just so happened that Medea was more than skilled in the magical arts. She would be a powerful ally for the Argonauts, but her heart was cold and withdrawn. Hera knew that only by a spell of love would Medea be willing to aid Jason and his men. Before the *Argo* ever touched the shores of Colchis, Hera had called upon Eros to stand by and remain close to the princess. When the opportune moment arrived, he would shoot Medea with an arrow of love, and from then on, she would be infatuated and deeply in love with the young prince.

When the Argonauts approached the city of Aia, they were given a royal escort to the court of King Aeetes, who welcomed the men as his most honored guests—well, that is until the king discovered the real reason the Argonauts had come to Colchis. Aeetes had half a mind to strike down the young prince right on the spot, but such acts were frowned upon in the democratic world of the ancient Greeks. Such actions often provoked generational blood feuds between kingdoms, and King Aeetes, for all his greed and faults, still cared for the peace and prosperity of his subjects.

That doesn't mean that the king was willing to give up his prized possession. Instead, he informed Jason that he was more than welcome to try his luck with defeating the dragon that guarded the cave, as well as the two fire-breathing bulls that Aeetes had added as extra security measures. Jason would need to tame both of the bulls. He would then need to use the animals to plow a giant field in which he would plant the teeth of a dragon. Those teeth would become soldiers, giant and merciless, and Jason would also need to slay them in order to claim his prize. And after all that, he needed to deal with the dragon guarding the fleece.

Jason could not refuse the king. He knew that if he did not take this challenge, he would be declared a thief, and King Aeetes would be well within his rights to cut down the hero where he stood and assign the Argonauts the same fate. Jason could forfeit his own life, but he would not make that choice for his men.

As Jason and Aeetes were discussing the terms of Jason's attempt to possess the golden fleece, Medea walked in. Eros was at the ready with an arrow already notched into his bow, and as soon as the main doors of the hall swung open for Medea to make her entrance, Eros shot her in the hip. Mortals did not feel the sting of Eros's arrows, so the princess continued forward without so much a stumble in her steps. When she lifted her eyes, the very first gaze she met was that of our hero Jason. Aeetes introduced his daughter, who was fairly lovely, with jet black hair and glowing dark eyes. In fact, Medea was hailed as being one of the most "bewitching" women of Greece. Her other distinguishing characteristic was her unyielding and ruthless nature, which was matched equally with her beauty. In psychological terms, the princess was borderline sociopathic. She was beautiful but crazy, and even with Eros's arrow of love still dug into her hip, no one could say for sure if her newfound love for Jason would match the love she had for herself. Eros wasn't going to leave anything to chance, so he also shot Jason for good measure.

Medea went to claim her seat next to her father's throne, and she held Jason's gaze for almost the entire time. As for Jason, he was having plenty of trouble focusing on the king and not his daughter. One final stipulation was that Jason would attempt to acquire the fleece on his own. He could not enlist the aid of his men. Jason was more than happy to accept those terms. He would need all of the Argonauts alive and well in order to row the ship back to Iolkos if he was to succeed in obtaining the fleece.

That night before Jason was to make his attempt, Medea visited him in his chambers. As Jason was lying in his bed, the princess seemed to evaporate through the walls. He never heard the door to his chambers open and close. She drifted to his side. No words were shared between the two lovers; they simply fell into one another's arms. Whilst lying in the afterglow of their love-making, Medea informed Jason that she was the only person who could ensure the success of his venture. Jason sat up and listened to his lover's proposal intently. Medea said that she would concoct an ointment that would protect him from the flames of the bulls. It would allow him to get close enough to tame and harness the animals, after which she would also help him soothe the dragon and tell him how to defeat the soldiers that would rise from its teeth.

However, Medea had some conditions of her own. She would not be willing to perform any of these tasks or divulge any information if Jason did not take her back to Iolkos and make her his queen. She assured Jason that without her help, he would surely die, leaving the hero very little choice. He also seemingly loved the princess, a side effect of Eros's arrow of love. How much he believed in her love, however, is not known. Nevertheless, he agreed to Medea's terms, and true to her word, she told Jason everything he needed to know in order to survive his perilous quest.

The next day, Jason bid his men farewell and ordered them to watch him from the cliffs above, all except the legendary and well-known musician Orpheus and Medea. She provided Jason with the ointment as promised. He slathered this all over his body before redressing and heading down to where the bulls lay in their field. Jason was able to approach the bulls, despite being consumed in a raging tunnel of hellfire. He made his way toward each animal, and after soft words and sweet nothings, he had both the bulls curled up at his feet like purring cats.

Jason Taming the Bulls of Aeëtes *by Jean-François de Troy, 1679–1752.*
(Public Domain; https://commons.wikimedia.org/wiki/File:Jean-Fran%C3%A7ois_de_Troy_-_Jason_Taming_the_Bulls_of_Ae%C3%ABtes,_1742.jpg

The next portion of the quest was to sow the dragon teeth. The teeth had already been harvested by Aeetes. With the teeth in hand, Jason went about plowing the field with the bulls and planting the teeth in orderly rows. Around a dozen soldiers clawed their way out of the earth. The night before, in Jason's chamber, Medea had assured her hero that what the soldiers possessed in brawn, they sorely lacked in brainpower. After all, these were not normal humans but things closer aligned with the laws of nature. These soldiers were provoked very easily since attack was their only mode of interaction. Thus, Jason threw rocks at the soldiers. Unaware that these stones were being hurled from far away, the soldiers engaged whomever they determined to be a threat, even those among their own brigade. In a matter of minutes, the soldiers had completely decimated one another. The only task left was for Jason to claim the fleece.

The dragon was all that was left. And this dragon never slept. As with most myths, there are different versions. For instance, some say that Medea had given Jason a concoction of herbs that put the dragon to sleep. However, a more exciting version exists. Orpheus, who was among the Argonauts, played a soothing lullaby with his harp. Medea even helped, using her sorcery to ensure the dragon fell asleep. Soon, the great and fearsome dragon was sleeping like a baby in no time. Music sometimes is really the only way to soothe a savage beast.

Once the beast was asleep, the three of them crept closer. Jason tiptoed around the slumbering dragon and found the fleece nailed to a tall but leafless tree bathed in a single ray of sunlight, which had broken through the top of the cave. Jason had never laid eyes on any material that was like the golden fleece. The very fibers seemed to beckon and seduce, which shows how King Aeetes lost his sanity and humanity in order to keep the fleece from the hands of other men. The three victors wasted no time in returning to the *Argo*, where the Argonauts were waiting, ready and prepared to set sail.

News of Jason's victory and hasty exit had made its way back to King Aeetes, who had never expected the young prince to succeed. He was instantly suspicious that someone in his family had aided Jason, but he surprisingly never considered Medea to be the culprit. She was his perfect little girl, and he didn't consider her capable of such treachery, although it was more than plausible to all who were aware of her true nature.

Aeetes called upon his firstborn son Apsyrtus to aid him in the hunt for the Argonauts. Aeetes no longer cared about public opinion or blood feuds; his anger clouded his judgment. The two of them set sail with their personal battalions and were just about to close in on their target. Meanwhile, Medea was below the deck of the *Argo*, performing blood magic in order to stop her father in his tracks. Medea cast a spell that caused a hemorrhage in her brother's brain. Apsyrtus fell onto his hands and knees, nauseous, his head throbbing. One of the soldiers called out to King Aeetes that his son was suffering, and the king immediately dashed to his son's side. But there was nothing that could be done.

The king's son collapsed, but this was not the worst to come. Medea's spell was twofold. While her brother suffered and was unable to comprehend time and space, he started to slowly disintegrate, similar to the appearance and infliction of leprosy. He was covered in boils and soars, but her spell sped up the disease. Before the king could do anything, his son had disintegrated completely, with all the blood from his body washing over the deck and pieces of flesh falling into the ocean. The grotesque and graphic sight halted the king's pursuit. He dared not follow the Argonauts any farther, for he feared that this torment had been delivered by a god. Medea was that powerful and that terrifying.

After a bout with the Sirens, the melodious flesh-eaters who lured men to their death with song, the Argonauts finally found refuge on the island of Drepane, where Jason and Medea were finally married. After a long rest on the island, Jason and the Argonauts made their way back to Iolkos, where the prince sought to finally claim his throne and rule as king. The entire company stormed into the throne room of the king, and Jason thrust the golden fleece at the feet of his uncle Pelias. However, Pelias would not relinquish his throne. With the golden fleece in hand, he could rule for decades and acquire new and very prominent lands. Why would he suddenly give up the throne to Jason now that he had both wealth and power?

Jason would not take this betrayal lying down. And he was even more willing to dispose of his uncle once he learned the truth from Medea that Pelias had murdered his father and caused his mother's heart to break to the point of death. Jason instructed Medea to exact revenge any way she could think, and Medea did not disappoint. One night in court, she gathered Pelias's daughters around her and told them that now their father had the fleece, he would become immortal. The daughters would now live under his sadistic and cruel rule for the rest of their lives. It was a little-known secret that Pelias was unwilling to let his daughters marry or relinquish control over their lives in any way. The girls were practically royal hostages. They could not bear the thought of their father outliving them, controlling their destinies until they were dead and gone. The three girls murdered Pelias and gave the throne willingly to Jason.

However, Jason had a huge problem on his hands. Once he had taken the throne and installed Medea as his queen, there were revolts throughout the kingdom. She was a well-known sorceress throughout the entirety of the Peloponnese, and she was greatly feared by those who knew the extent of her power and ruthless nature. The people of Iolkos would not have a foreign sorceress as their queen. Jason, fearing for the safety of his beloved wife and protector, took her away into exile on the island of Corinth, where he planned to live out the rest of their days in joy and happiness together.

They were happy enough for some time. Medea even gave birth to three of Jason's children. However, soon after they were born, Jason fell from grace. One night, he approached Medea and asked her permission to propose marriage to the princess of Corinth. All things considered, it was actually unwise for Jason to make this request. Medea was just as possessive of Jason as she was protective, and his request to be with another woman was the ultimate betrayal in her eyes. Jason loved her, but she could be cold and unforgiving, and yet, he believed that she would never bring him to harm. As cliché as it is, hell hath no fury like a woman scorned, and Medea had no interest in sharing her husband with another princess. For Jason to even make this request was a great offense, and the only thing she could think of was revenge.

She killed the princess of Corinth, causing her to go mad and fling herself from the highest cliff on the island. If this wasn't enough, to further punish Jason, she massacred their three young children and laid each one in their marital bed for her husband to find. Once her revenge was complete, she made her way to Athens to seek the throne of another king.

Jason returned home later that evening to find the last joys of his life, his beloved children, slaughtered to the point that they were almost unrecognizable. The loss of a child is the deepest despair. The greatest of all mortal heroes, who had traveled the seas, bested the most fearsome creatures of the ancient world, and won back his crown only to relinquish it for love, was undone by the same ruthless woman he took to be his bride. Jason lived out the rest of his days alone. He had even lost the favor of Hera for breaking his vow to Medea. He died when one of the beams of the *Argo* fell and hit him in the head. Jason died instantly, buried in the ruins of one of the greatest ships to ever sail the seas and as one of the greatest heroes that ever lived.

Chapter Eleven – Theseus: The Minotaur Slayer

So, you remember how the queen of Crete had been impregnated by the most beautiful bull of all time, the Cretan Bull? From their bestial union came the Minotaur, who would become the terror of Crete. King Minos placed his wife's terrible offspring in a giant labyrinth underneath his palace and began to feed this beast with prisoners and his enemies. Although it was an effective method of implementing fear into his people and disposing of traitors, it didn't exactly leave the right message with the remaining kings of Greece or the king's own subjects. The cannibalistic nature of the Minotaur was disturbing enough, let alone a king who actively sated such a beast. Minos was the same sort of detestable enemy that Herakles went up against in his twelve labors, Diomedes (the king who was feeding human parts to his mares).

These sacrifices soothed King Minos's great shame that his wife had cheated on him with a divine bull. Soon enough, the Minotaur would have more than the enemies of the king to consume. However, the mythology of the Minotaur begins with a king who yearned for a son and a princess who managed to sleep with not only a king but a god and all in a single evening.

Years before the sexual encounter of Queen Pasiphae and the Cretan Bull, the king of Athens, Aegeus, was about to reach his early thirties and still had not managed to have a son. On a diplomatic mission to the kingdom of Troezen, he told the king of his concerns to produce an heir. The good king offered his daughter Aethra for Aegeus to bed for the evening, thinking that perhaps from their union, a son would be produced. The two young lovers (if we can even call them that) spent the night together. Later, slumbering in the afterglow of some decent love-making, the princess had a strange dream—a very strange dream. The goddess Athena appeared to Aethra and told her that the child who would grow in her belly from this night would be an exceptionally blessed child, one destined to perform great and heroic deeds. Athena told the princess to go down to the sea, stand near the water's edge, and wait. Aethra rose from her place in bed and followed the goddess's instructions.

She waited by the edge of the sea, the small waves gently kissing her toes. Although the sources are somewhat hazy, it is possible that the princess was not entirely conscious during her visit to the water; it was as if she was in a state of hypnosis. Right on cue, the god of the seas, Poseidon, emerged from the dark water and proceeded to have sex with the princess. When it comes to producing ideal heroes, the gods and goddesses of Olympus really don't pay attention to things like consent, but most of the mythology surrounding this particular tale makes it evident that the princess indeed enjoyed herself both back in the palace with Aegeus and on the beach that same night with Poseidon.

Oftentimes in Greek mythology, it was not uncommon for one child to have two fathers or two mothers or to be conceived in the stomach of a woman but then placed in the thigh of a man for the rest of the gestation period. The rules of science don't apply when we are talking about divine sperm. So, as mythology would have it, from this double union was born the hero Theseus. His claim as the son of Aegeus gave him lands, a title, and power. His godly patrilineage also gave him abilities that were not common to the world of mortal men. Since his birth was also blessed and orchestrated in some sense by the goddess Athena, Theseus would also have a logical mind, one unclouded by fear and able to rationally calculate the best course of action for success. All these qualities and more would serve him well when he reached manhood and had to fulfill a task that etched his name in the stone of Greek legends.

The next morning after Aegeus spent the night with the daughter of the king (he was unaware of her little late-night visit to the beach), he made preparations to return to Athens. However, before he departed, he left something behind for his future son. Near the same spot where Aethra had lain with Poseidon, Aegeus placed his sword and sandals under a large smooth stone. When his son came of age, Aegeus hoped that he would find the objects and return to Athens with these tools to take his rightful place as prince.

So, Theseus grew up in Troezen with his mother, and when he turned seventeen, she took him down to the water's edge and told him the story of his conception. When the princess had finished speaking, she took her son to the stone where his father's possessions had been stored for nearly two decades. Theseus, a strong youth at this point, rolled away the stone with great ease. His quest to reach Athens and claim his birthright had begun, as did the legend of Theseus and the Minotaur.

Before Theseus set out on his journey, his mother Aethra begged him to go by way of the sea and not to travel on the road. In the ancient world, when you traveled on the open road, it was a dangerous undertaking, one that included thieves who wouldn't think twice about slicing your throat and making off with your possessions. Or even worse, some sort of otherworldly creature could rip your eyeballs from their sockets or flay you alive. Of course, there were threats on the open waters, but Theseus, determined to prove himself worthy of his parentage, decided to travel by road. Armed with the king's sword, Theseus set out, and along the way, he encountered his fair share of trials and victories. He killed every foe he met on the road. These were not innocent travelers but evil men and monsters, defilers of human life. They were feared by many and challenged by none until the young prince arrived.

The first evildoer he encountered was a man who went by the name of Periphetes. This brute was known for bashing in the skulls of travelers with his iron club. What's worse is he didn't steal anything from his victims; the killings were purely for sport. Theseus managed to kill Periphetes, and he took his weapon as a trophy. Also, it wasn't every day that one came across such a fine weapon. The next man Theseus came up against was a far more sick and twisted individual than Periphetes; he was known as the stretcher or Procrustes. This disturbed individual would tie his victims to an iron bed and proceed to stretch their limbs so that they reached the edges of the bed. The unfortunate souls, who were too tall for the bed, would have their limbs chopped off one by one, a hand there, a foot here, until Procrustes was satisfied with the physical dimensions of the torture. Theseus came up against the stretcher and cleaved him in half with his sword.

By this point in his journey, word had begun to reach certain cities in Greece of Theseus's heroic accomplishments. When he arrived in Athens to finally stand before his father, the hero encountered more danger. A few years after his night with the princess of Troezen, King Aegeus had remarried, taking the sorceress and ex-wife of Jason, Medea, as his bride. This was a woman who liked to be in control of her fate and those around her at all times. She knew that her husband awaited the return of his son, and she feared that her claim to rule and influence Aegeus would wane.

When Theseus arrived in the throne room of the king, Medea, being wily in her ways and more than willing to kill for her station, convinced Aegeus that their new visitor could not be trusted. She whispered in his ear to give the young man a cup of poison to drink. It was better safe than sorry. Aegeus offered the drink to his son, unbeknownst of his true identity until the moment Theseus stepped forward to accept the drink. As he took a step toward the king, his sword swung into view. King Aegeus recognized the weapon immediately. This was his son and long-awaited heir. Medea couldn't run out of that throne room fast enough, and she fled to an unknown location.

The reunion between the king and his son was one overflowing with joy. Not long after that, however, their joy was stifled by the unfortunate political situation between Athens and Crete. Before Theseus had arrived, Aegeus had hosted a series of games with all of the neighboring Greek *poleis*. In one of the events, the son of King Minos, Androgeus, was crushed by a runaway chariot. King Minos was so outraged by the unexpected death of his young son that he demanded tribute from Athens. In order to avoid a war with the irrational king of Crete, Aegeus consented to King Minos's idea of reparations. Every year, the city of Athens sent fourteen of the most beautiful and virtuous young men and women to be given in sacrifice to the great terror of Crete, the Minotaur. The ship that ferried the tributes to the island always sailed under a black flag so that passing ships would know that sacrifices were aboard.

When Theseus discovered that his father had essentially been politically forced into such barbary, he decided to put an end to the Minotaur. His plan was to offer himself as a tribute and go into the maze and slay the beast. When he informed his father of his plan, the king would not hear of it. His only son would be sailing toward his potential death. Aegeus had only just welcomed his much-awaited heir back into his life. However, after much debating and convincing, the king finally consented to his son's quest but made him swear that when he was sailing back to Athens, he would raise white sails on his ship, replacing the black sails of death. This way, the king would know his son had survived and was returning home.

So, the day of tribute came, and true to his word, Theseus offered himself up. This was a most special tribute indeed, for the long-lost prince was the prized jewel of Athens. He was the most lovely, the most strong, and the most intelligent youth that Aegeus could offer. Minos was very pleased when he received word that one of Greece's most powerful kings was consenting to let his only son be devoured by an unholy monster. When Theseus stepped off the ship in Crete, he and the other tributes were led up to the palace of the king to be inspected.

King Minos greeted his royal guest, shaking his hand. He then presented him to his young daughter Ariadne, who was immediately struck by Theseus's beauty and charm. The young prince also noted Ariadne's striking beauty. Later that night, the princess visited Theseus in the tribute's quarters, and the two shared a passionate night together. Theseus confided in the princess and told her of his plan to slay the Minotaur. Although he seemed confident in his abilities to succeed in his quest, Ariadne knew that even if he managed to kill the beast, he would most certainly get lost in the maze. Many tributes had died not by a direct attack from the Minotaur but from succumbing to starvation or dehydration. Their corpses lined the walls of the maze and acted as snacks for the beast to devour later.

Early the next morning, Ariadne awoke before anyone else in the palace. She went down to the docks, where she collected a spool of thread from one of the vendors and returned to the bed of Theseus. She woke her love and instructed him to take the spool with him into the maze. Before he entered, he needed to tie the end of the thread to one of the columns just outside the entrance when he was alone. The guards who manned the maze never followed the tributes all the way inside. They were terrified of the Minotaur and for a good reason. The beast did not distinguish between friend or foe, prey or master. If King Minos walked into the maze, he would be treated no differently than the tributes. This spool would act as Theseus's bread crumbs, leading him back to safety once he had slain the Minotaur. Ariadne also managed to obtain a sword for her love and hid it near the entrance. For all Ariadne had done to help, Theseus promised to take her back with him to Athens.

And so, Theseus and the other Athenian tributes were pushed into the dark passageways of the maze. The stench was worse than anything Theseus could have imagined. The decaying corpses and bones of the Minotaur's previous meals were strewn about, shreds of ripped skin clinging to the walls, which were splattered brown with the dried blood of hundreds of victims. The twists and turns of the passageways were sporadic, and the walls seemed to move and change direction at will. The darkness in the labyrinth was all-consuming. The naked human eye couldn't make out more than two to three feet in front of them, but thankfully, not all of the tributes in the maze were all human. As a demi-god, Theseus possessed heightened senses, natural reflexes, and intuitions that allowed him to be on par with the Minotaur in terms of strength and speed.

He couldn't see in the dark, but the air in the labyrinth was thick and cold. Theseus could feel the changes in tension, and he proceeded into the blackness slowly, Ariadne's string tied to his hip. He wasn't the hunted; he was the hunter. For nearly two hours, Theseus listened and walked the maze while trying to make out the faintest sounds and changes in the environment. The rest of the tributes had stayed near the early portions of the maze, hoping they wouldn't encounter the beast.

A mosaic of Theseus and the Minotaur.
(Public Domain;
https://commons.wikimedia.org/wiki/File:Theseus_Minotaur_Mosaic.jpg)

Theseus eventually stopped searching and decided to make the Minotaur come to him. He began to bang his sword on the wall every so often so that the beast could get a sense of where he was but not pinpoint his exact location. Then Theseus heard it: the distinct clip-clop of a bovine hoof. The stench intensified. The strength of the Minotaur's breath seemed to change the air temperature around Theseus as well, even though he could tell the beast was at least several feet away from him. Theseus stood fast, his hand on the hilt of his sword, ready for the moment the beast charged him with its great horns.

The Minotaur stamped its foot on the ground once, twice. It ran right at the young prince, who unsheathed his weapon at the last minute. With one graceful strike, he buried his blade in the Minotaur's neck. The beast, still in shock over the deadly assault, was still trying to run forward, further impaling himself on Theseus's blade until the point broke through the back of his skull. The great terror of King Minos and the island of Crete had been defeated. Theseus chopped off the Minotaur's head for good measure, taking it as a trophy for his father, and proceeded to follow his safety line all the way out of the labyrinth with the other Athenian tributes, who were all alive and well.

Ariadne couldn't control her happiness when she saw that the man of her dreams was alive. Although Theseus was the main actor in this tale, it was Ariadne who had ensured his survival. Without her brilliant idea, Theseus would have been walking toward his death, and he knew it. He, Ariadne, and the tributes stole away on the ship with black sails and set out for Athens. However, all was not right in paradise, as they say. The ship stopped at the island of Naxos to resupply, and the next morning when Ariadne awoke, she found herself sleeping alone on the beach. Dumbstruck by her situation, she scoured the length of the beach for her love, then looked inland to see if she could see the Athenians up high on the terrain. "Perhaps they were searching for more food or water?" she told herself, but she knew it was a lie. The young princess slowly turned toward the sea and saw the black sails on the horizon. There was Theseus on board his ship, sailing away from the island, the tributes in tow.

Why would he abandon the princess? The myths are a bit hazy with this one. It is thought that jealous Hera had appeared to the Athenian prince in a dream and convinced him to leave the young woman behind. Some say Dionysus wanted Ariadne for himself right then and convinced Theseus to leave her. However, it is also possible that Theseus realized he did not care for Ariadne as much as he thought. Perhaps he was just using her, or perhaps he did not want to spend the rest of his life with her as his queen. Despite being revered as heroes, many demi-gods made a great deal of questionable moral decisions. This was usually done to comment on their human side and their tendency toward imperfection. Demigod or not, Theseus was still a man. Poor Ariadne was not devastated for long because shortly after her abandonment, she was seduced by Dionysus, who carried her off to become his wife and the mother to two of his children.

On his way back to Athens, Theseus began to regret abandoning the princess. He realized that perhaps he did love Ariadne. He was so distraught over losing a woman he deliberately left on an island that he forgot to change the sails on his ship from black to white, which would indicate to his father that he had survived the terrible ordeal and was returning home. King Aegeus had lookouts posted on the cliffs day and night for the last fortnight so that he would be notified the moment Theseus's ship was spotted. One of the lookouts noticed a black spot coming toward the cliffs, but he couldn't make out if it was the prince or an enemy ship. Eventually, he was able to identify the black sails. The lookout ran all the way to the palace and burst through the doors into the throne room. He threw himself before the feet of the king and wept that black sails had been spotted on the water.

The king, in disbelief, rushed to the cliffs and indeed saw that the watcher had spoken truthfully. There is little despair in this world that is equivalent to the death of a child. Aegeus had lost his son and, therefore, his heart and will to live. The king couldn't bear the pain. Without hesitation, he stepped off the edge of the cliff into the open air below. Theseus saw his father as he impaled himself on the rocks below and was heartbroken for the second time. He was now the king of Athens, but it was a throne he took filled with grief and sorrow. As a demi-god, Theseus was strong and brave, but he lost his love and his father all in one day because of his weakness as a man.

Chapter Twelve – Perseus and Medusa

The story of the demi-god Perseus begins with the love affair of his parents. Although Zeus had many wives and even more lovers, the man was a very emotional creature. He was a person who fell in love with everything and everyone. It has been said that out of all those women, he loved Danae the best. She was the daughter of King Acrisius and Queen Eurydice, and she was beloved by her people but feared by her father. For years, the king and queen had failed to produce a son to inherit the throne. When their daughter was finally born, their joy was unparalleled, but a dark and disturbing thought had dwelled in the king's mind for years over this very event.

Before Danae was conceived, Acrisius had sought the counsel and divination of the Pythian oracle to determine whether he would ever have a son. Perhaps he had angered or offended the gods in some manner but did not realize it? The oracle informed the desperate king that his line would indeed produce a male heir, but it would not be his. The child would one day grow to dispose of Acrisius and bring ruin to all he loved and held dear. Shortly after Danae was born, Acrisius realized it would be her womb that produced his downfall. When Danae bled for the first time, her father wasted no time in shutting her in a subterranean room entirely made of stone and earth. There was little to no light that reached the princess, save for a skylight above with metal bars over the gap.

Danae stayed there for two winters. Another person would have given up all hope that they would ever leave; maybe, they would succumb to the loneliness and desperation they felt. But not Danae. She somehow never lost her hope in that dark and secluded cell. Zeus had been listening to the girl's prayers. She was strong and stoic, and Zeus fell in love with her gentle yet relentless spirit. One night, he visited her in that prison, coming down through the spaces between the skylight bars as golden rain. In this form, he made love to Danae.

The experience for Zeus was also something different, and when his wife Hera inquired about the reason behind his infidelity, "Zeus who gathers the clouds answered her [Hera]: 'Never before has love for any goddess or woman so melted about the heart inside me, broken it to submission, as now: not that time...when I loved Akrisios' [Acrisius's] daughter sweet-stepping Danaë.'"[2] This would have been hurtful for Hera to hear, but one can assume that Zeus was telling the truth. Zeus had some despicable tendencies, but this sounds like unbridled honesty.

That night brought about the birth of Perseus. Danae gave birth in her cell alone. After her labor was complete, her father wasted no time in disposing of her and her newborn child. After the king's physician had certified Danae's son, Acrisius commissioned his masons to build a sarcophagus. He placed his young daughter and grandson in it and cast the two out to sea.

Zeus had been keeping watch over Danae since she fell pregnant, and as soon as she was tossed into the waves, Poseidon

---

[2] Homer, *Iliad* 14. 319 ff, trans. Lattimore. [Greek epic, c. 8th BCE]

was at the ready. He carried the sarcophagus safely to the ship of a fisherman by the name of Dictys. He ferried her safely to the island of Seriphos, a small and secluded kingdom. Still, word gets around. For the first few days after her arrival, Dictys nursed the young mother back to health. She mostly slept, waking only to nurse her child; Dictys handled everything else. The fisherman had lost his own wife and child years prior, so seeing Danae in this condition broke his heart. He did not want the woman and her young son to be without support, something which he could not provide in his meager surroundings. This child needed a father or at the very least some direct guidance, and his mother, being a single mother and a vulnerable woman, needed the protection of someone in power, someone like his brother, King Polydectes.

Although Dictys had good intentions, his brother did not possess the same kind and generous spirit. He yearned for Danae, and after the king made several advances, all of which Danae turned down, he decided the solution was to kidnap her and lock her away while still trying to court the poor woman. One captivity in a lifetime was more than enough, but Danae was destined to suffer. As for her young son, Polydectes was merciful, to a degree, and sent Perseus off to be raised in the temple of Athena.

In actuality, this was one of the most generous things he could have done for the young hero, for it was the beginning of Perseus's patronage and favor with the goddess Athena. She would later become an indispensable part of his story. Years later, when Perseus had reached manhood, he returned to the house of his former foster father, Dictys, and lamented over the captivity of his mother. Dictys informed the young hero to go before the king and demand the release of his mother. Dictys knew that the king would not let her go willingly and would set before Perseus an impossible task in exchange for his mother's release. Dictys, however, was not entirely unaware of Perseus's lineage. Danae had confided in Dictys like a father, having been so estranged from what should have been the natural love of her own biological dad. She had informed him of that night in her cell when she was impregnated with Perseus. Whatever challenge Polydectes set before the demi-god, Perseus would surely succeed.

When Perseus stepped into the throne room of the king, he saw his mother sitting at Polydectes's feet, chained to the floor. She had changed, as the weariness and turmoil of her circumstances had dulled her spirit, but she was still beautiful. Perseus had to stop himself from rushing to embrace her. It angered and hurt him to see his beautiful and brave mother in such a fashion. Whatever the obstacle, Perseus would complete his task one way or another or find a way to kill the king.

He demanded the release of his mother, and Polydectes agreed to comply if and only if Perseus would go on a quest for the head of the legendary and fearsome Gorgon Medusa. Remember her? She had been raped by Poseidon and then maliciously cursed by Athena, the goddess of wisdom and rationality. Medusa had to live the rest of her days with snakes for hair and a gaze that turned any living creature into stone. Perseus consented to kill the Gorgon or die trying, and he turned to leave the throne room. He looked back only once to catch the glance of his mother's eyes, rimmed with tears yet stoic and bluer than the Aegean Sea.

Zeus, who had been following the escapades of his son and former lover since the day Perseus was conceived, beseeched the gods and goddesses of Olympus to aid Perseus in his quest and to bestow upon him gifts that would help him to slay the Gorgon. Hades selflessly gave Perseus his very own helmet of invisibility. The mighty Hephaestus forged a steel sword with a golden handle for the young hero. Athena presented him with a reflective bronze shield, and Hermes gifted him a pair of winged sandals. All of these gifts would be necessary for Perseus to best Medusa, who was well equipped with the best defense mechanism of any man or animal. On top of this, she was also a gifted archer. Not to mention she had years of pent-up aggression and rage toward the world of men and gods for her current predicament.

After collecting his gifts from the gods and bidding farewell to Dictys, Perseus set out on his quest for Medusa's head. For starters, getting to the dwelling of Medusa would be a trip and a half. Her cave was located deep beneath Mt. Olympus in caverns that were as old as the original Titans. Medusa would not be the only foul creature lurking in those dark passageways and halls made of stone. Eventually, Perseus found his way to the entrance of her cave. Mastering all of his courage, he entered the darkness. The coils and hisses of serpents were his guides for finding Medusa, and lucky for him, when he did find her, she was fast asleep. The hero finding his hunted target in a deep slumber was not unusual in Greek mythology. Certain versions of Theseus and the Minotaur recount how Theseus found the beast asleep and was able to kill it with great ease. Even asleep and with her eyes closed, though, Medusa was dangerous. Perseus did not want to chance anything, as a non-direct gaze could have the same full blast radius of a wide-awake Gorgon.

He turned his back to face the monster and held up his shield to use as a mirror in order to locate Medusa. Carefully stepping backward, he lifted his sword high in the air and brought it crashing down at the base of Medusa's neck. The decapitated monster wiggled and wretched as her head went rolling away from her body. From her severed neck sprouted her twins, Pegasus and Chrysaor. The former would become Perseus's personal mount, and he would be crucial for the success of his remaining quest.

Perseus did not move a muscle, and he wouldn't open his eyes until he heard complete silence. Once Medusa's body had stopped involuntarily convulsing, Perseus used his shield again to find her severed head and laid his cloak over it for good measure. He then wrapped it up, chucked it in his satchel, mounted the winged steed Pegasus, and began to fly back to the island of Seriphos to free his mother from her captor.

Perseus with the Head of Medusa *by Benvenuto Cellini, 1554.*
(Credit: Xosema, CC BY-SA 4.0 via Wikimedia Commons;
https://commons.wikimedia.org/wiki/File:Florencia_-_Firenze_-
_Perseo_con_la_cabeza_de_Medusa_-_Benvenuto_Cellini_-_01.jpg)

On the way back, our hero encountered another damsel in distress, Andromeda, the daughter of King Cepheus and Queen Cassiopeia, who were lords of Joppa in the Levant. Some say that the king and queen were the rulers of Ethiopia, but their origins were not from mainland Greece or the surrounding Greek islands. At a party one evening, the queen had boasted arrogantly that her daughter was the most beautiful creature in the world. Her boasting got worse and worse until she crossed a line mere mortals dare not cross. She exclaimed that her beloved child was even more lovely than the Nereids, the nymph daughters of Poseidon. Various versions of the story interchange the object of her offense, for sometimes it is Aphrodite or Thetis, but the bottom line is that she greatly offended the immortals.

As punishment, the god Poseidon threatened to destroy the city of Joppa by unleashing the monstrous Cetus, a sea creature and the doomed spawn of Poseidon himself. Poseidon, who was perhaps the least merciful of the gods, provided the king and queen with one method of saving their beloved kingdom and all the innocent souls under their dominion. He instructed them to sacrifice their one and only child to Cetus by chaining her onto a rock in the Mediterranean Sea. Only her blood would sate Cetus and save the city.

Now, any sort of political choice is not made lightly and always presents a few cons and pros, either of which can tip the scales toward a certain decision. The decision that King Cepheus and Queen Cassiopeia reached was that the life of their city was worth more than that of their daughter. They were young, and the queen's womb was still functioning, but replacing a city and their people would be nearly impossible after a divine and very aggressive sea monster virtually wiped them clean from the face of the earth. Andromeda also cared about the life and safety of her people, so she willingly allowed herself to be led down to the shore and strapped to the boulder to await her fate as the martyr of Joppa.

Perseus was flying by at the time and saw the fair maiden upon the rock. At first, he took no great notice of her predicament, but as he flew closer, he saw the fair beauty of the maiden and then the rolling waves that seemed to grow larger and larger as they approached the princess. Finally, Cetus's head broke the surface of the water, and out he sprang from the sea, a gigantic serpent. His slimy form crawled its way onto the shore, ready to devour the tender princess. Perseus immediately recognized the danger, and he knew what he must do to stop the monster and save the princess. No creature made of flesh and blood was a match for the stone-cold gaze of a Gorgon's severed head, most of all, the severed head of the deadliest Gorgon in all the ancient world.

Perseus dive-bombed his winged steed, and as he descended, he whipped out the terrifying head, readying himself to face it toward Cetus. When the sea dragon made eye contact with Medusa's head, it immediately began to recoil and retract, unable to comprehend the ice-cold feeling seeping its way into its veins and muscular tissues. Fear gripped the serpent and shone from the hollow yellow in its bright eyes, which were the last body parts to be rendered motionless and dead for all time. Legend has it that Cetus can still be found in his stone form in the ancient Levant somewhere near the Red Sea, while others say it is at the edge of the Mediterranean.

Perseus cut Andromeda down from her boulder, loaded her up onto Pegasus, and flew to the castle to demand her hand in marriage from her parents. The king and queen would have immediately obliged, given the fact that the rescuer was the answer to their prayers for having saved not only their beloved daughter but also their fair city. However, their daughter's hand was already promised to another. This did not seem to faze Perseus, and he asked the king and queen to bring forth the inconsequential prince. Perseus saw that the prince was a weak and cruel man who resented Perseus for having been the one to rescue his betrothed.

Perseus wasted no time and pulled forth Medusa's head from his bloody satchel. The prince didn't even have time to scream before he, too, was turned to stone. The king and queen were more or less elated, if not slightly terrified, of their soon-to-be son-in-law. Perseus and Andromeda headed back to Seriphos to finally rescue Perseus's mother from her own non-consensual marriage, one bonded not in love but with chains.

Perseus had to be cunning. He knew that his mother would be sitting at her designated place of imprisonment, at the feet of King Polydectes. He first went to see his adoptive father, Dictys, both to say hello and to help him concoct a plan to set his mother free.

Upon seeing that Perseus was not only alive and well but also victorious in his quest and married to the lovely Andromeda, Dictys wept with happiness. Dictys said that he would request Danae come visit him at his home to help mend some old fishing nets. Danae usually came by herself when she visited Dictys, so he knew his brother would be alone in the throne room.

On the day of Danae's visit, unbeknownst to her, Perseus walked into the throne room to present Medusa's head to the king as he requested. Polydectes was floored. He did not expect Perseus to survive his quest, and he was thankful that his mother was not there to see that her son had succeeded. Polydectes was already thinking of ways to have Perseus killed before his mother could ever discover that he had returned. Before he could even get out a greeting to his stepson, Perseus revealed the severed head of the Gorgon and turned the king to stone right there on his throne. For good measure, Perseus came up behind the stone king and pushed him off the throne, causing the statue to shatter into a million pieces. This was the end of the malignant Polydectes. Few would mourn the evil king.

When Danae returned to the throne room, she saw her own son sitting on the throne with his new queen beside him. Few mothers in the history of the ancient world felt such unparalleled joy and relief at seeing their son. Danae must have gasped in happiness, for her son was not only alive but had also inherited the keys to the kingdom. It is typical of ancient tales, whether they are considered to be mythological, biblical, or otherwise, to end with the death of a most beloved son or the parent. The story of Perseus and Medusa is one of the rare exceptions where the hero and parent are reunited in a happy ending.

Chapter Thirteen: The Trojan War

The *Iliad* and the *Aeneid*, which recount the story of the Trojan War, are some of the most circulated stories in the modern world. Thousands of years after its inception, the tale of the Trojan War still captivates readers with its lessons of human flaws, strengths, desires, and hopes. The characters' names and personas have been elevated in the pages of history and mythology for their unique sense of telling the story of many. For instance, who of us hasn't felt the sting of unrequited love? Plus, some people are just really unlucky. The sense of triumph and travesty that is accessible to every human being can be found in the pages of the *Iliad* and the *Aeneid*.

As we expressed earlier in this book, the main subject of a Greek myth never begins with the story itself but with a few others instead. Context and background were very important to the Greeks. Who one was depended on where one came from, and their circumstances eventually trickled down into a single destiny. The rest of the story was dictated by one's choices.

The story of the Trojan War begins with the wedding of Peleus and Thetis, the parents of the hero and legendary fighter Achilles (you know you're a major influence on the world when a whole portion of the ankle is named after you and your story, but more on that later). Thetis was the daughter of the second-generation Titan Nereus and his nymph-goddess wife, Doris. Together, the two had fifty daughters, the eldest of which was Thetis. She looked after her sisters and, like her parents, could shapeshift into any marine creature. The family inhabited a series of sea caves buried deep within the underbelly of the Aegean, and there they remained, peaceful and relatively undisturbed.

That was until the day that Peleus struck a bargain with Zeus for the hand of Thetis, the loveliest and adored of her sisters. The Oracle of Delphi had prophesized that Thetis's son would be twice as great as his sire. Zeus could not allow himself to succumb to Thetis's charms, nor could he allow any of the other immortals the chance to have her as their wife or lover. The child that would come from her womb could be powerful enough to kill them all and disrupt the world order. Thus, Zeus plotted to have her betrothed to a mortal man. This was when Peleus, the king of Phthia, stepped onto the scene. He was powerful enough to be respectable but would not produce a son greater than the gods.

His child, however, would still be considered a demi-god, given his mother's impressive divine lineage, and would make a name for himself as one of the greatest fighters the world had ever seen. Although demi-gods typically are not immortal beings and are by no means 100 percent invincible, they can succumb to death and injury given the right circumstances. To ensure her son retained some of her invincibility as an immortal, Thetis took him to the River Styx when he was a small child. She held her baby by one of his heels and dipped his entire body into the waters of the dead. However, the spot where she had held Achilles did not enter the water. His heel was his only weak spot. How Achilles was able to survive being submerged in the river is largely debated. Usually, those with any mortal heritage who fell into the river would not survive, hence the need for a boatman to ferry the souls of the dead into the underworld.

The wedding of Peleus and Thetis was a very joyous affair, and all of the immortals were invited to the wedding except for Eris, the goddess of discord. Despite not receiving an invitation for obvious reasons, the goddess still took the decision to heart. All things considered, it was unwise for the happy couple to disrespect her in such a manner and not expect some kind of retaliation in return. Eris devised a plan to ruin the wedding festivities. She sent a golden apple to the feast as a wedding present, and she addressed it to "the most beautiful of all the goddesses."

Naturally, Hera, Athena, and Aphrodite all thought they had a claim to the apple. Zeus sent the apple, along with the three goddesses, to the city of Troy, where the goddesses would be judged by the young Prince Paris. "Let the hands of men be soiled with this unpopular decision," thought Zeus. Paris was damned if he didn't judge and damned if he did. He had no way of knowing just how much his decision would affect the rest of his kingdom and change the face of the Greek world for all time.

The goddesses approached Paris when he was out one morning hunting with his guards. He came to a large clearing with one tall olive tree right in the middle. The area was completely silent, and Paris climbed down from his horse to collect a few of the beautiful olives. Suddenly, he heard another party make their way into the clearing. Hand on his sword, ready for any friend or foe, he turned quickly and was shocked to see three goddesses standing before him. Paris fell to his knees. Each goddess offered him a gift if he declared her the most beautiful. All the goddesses offered generous gifts, but Paris was persuaded by Aphrodite's enticing offer. At the end of the day, she was the best judge amongst the three goddesses as to what the prince's heart truly desired. She offered him the hand of the most beautiful woman in the world: Helen, the reigning queen of Sparta. This was obviously an issue, but the fact that Helen belonged to another man did not dissuade the young prince from claiming his prize.

Paris made the journey to Sparta under the false pretense of a political mission to discuss the terms of imports and exports with the Spartan king, Menelaus, a great warrior who came from a prominent royal family. His brother, Agamemnon, was the king of Mycenae, and he was on a political quest to unite and rule over all the *poleis* of Greece. Although each Greek city-state had its own particular ruler or king, it was Agamemnon who declared that all of these men would answer to him and be at his beck and call for any sort of need. It was a position that required a great deal of strength and strategy. Paris was playing with fire by seeking to abduct the beautiful wife of Agamemnon's favorite brother.

When Paris walked into the throne room, Menelaus greeted the young prince with open arms and orchestrated a whole banquet in his honor, not knowing that he had just invited a snake to dinner. As for Helen, she was immediately smitten with the young prince's handsome features and fine manners. (Some accounts say she did not care for Paris in the same way he did or that Aphrodite intervened to make sure they loved each other; we chose to go with the romantic version.) Her current husband, Menelaus, could be a cold and brutish warrior without the finer subtleties and touch of a man that a woman of Helen's status preferred. Although Menelaus loved Helen and vice versa, there was a certain spark of passion missing. According to some accounts, Helen was just a prize to Menelaus, a beautiful jewel to make other men more envious of his stature and position. It only took a few encounters for Helen and Paris to be absolutely enthralled with one another. After about a month of their affair, it was time for Paris to sail back to Troy.

Little did Menelaus know that below the deck of the Trojan ship was his prized bride. When he discovered that Helen was missing from her chambers, he went ballistic. He had no idea where she could have gone until a fisherman came to the court of the king and revealed that he had seen her board the ship and share a kiss with the young prince the night before the Trojans were to set sail.

Upon their arrival in Troy, King Priam, Paris's father, and Prince Hector, Paris's older brother, were outraged at what the young prince had done. However, it was too late to undo the wrong that had been done. Even if Helen was returned, it was not in Menelaus's nature to forgive, and Paris would have met an unfortunate death regardless. Who knows what ills and abuse would have been done to Helen? Priam was a soft-hearted king who ruled and commanded respect and power through his wisdom and kindness. He loved his sons dearly and would never wish them to come to any harm despite their mistakes or failings.

While Helen was being greeted by the entirety of the Trojan court and nobles, Menelaus was sailing to Mycenae to request the help of his brother in a campaign against Troy. They would sail to the city, reclaim Menelaus's wife, and lay waste to the entire city. Agamemnon willingly agreed. Men with all the power in the world usually only care about one thing: gaining more power. Agamemnon cared very little for his brother's pretty little wife, but he cared very much for the stature and power provided in decimating perhaps the greatest city in Anatolia, which is now present-day Turkey. This was already shaping up to be one of the most legendary wars in Greek history, and Agamemnon sought the allegiance of some of the greatest kings and warriors of all time. His list included Odysseus, king of Ithaca; Ajax the Great, a descendant of Zeus and the cousin of Achilles; and, as one might have guessed, the brave and fearsome Achilles himself.

Over one thousand ships set sail for the coast of Turkey. Achilles commanded his own ship and a force of specialized soldiers, the Myrmidons, which were widely acknowledged as the most fearsome men in Greece. These soldiers would do anything their general asked without delay. Also sailing with Achilles was his best friend and most trusted advisor Patroclus.

For the first few years of the war, all of the battles were evenly matched, with plenty of casualties on both sides. Hector, being the eldest prince of Troy, always led his army onto the battlefield. He was also one of the most skilled warriors Troy had ever seen, and he even held his own against Ajax the Great. Hector was guarded by Apollo during this battle, and Athena chose Ajax as her champion. Even the gods took sides in the war. Apollo was the patron god of Troy. He would always look out for members of the royal family, as the city of Troy had maintained his patronage for hundreds of years, currying his favor with gifts and sacrifices of immense worth. When their dance of death was over, both men greatly respected the other. Hector presented his sword to Ajax to honor the hero's great skill and speed; Ajax would later use this sword to kill himself.

One battle ended in great tragedy for Achilles. At one point during the war, Achilles is upset with Agamemnon. The great king had taken his slave, Briseis, for his own, even though Achilles was the one to enslave her. He refused to fight as a result, which was devastating for the Greeks since he was one of their strongest fighters. But unless his prize was returned to him, he would not go on the battlefield.

Although the Greeks entreat him to fight, showering him with promises of wealth and the return of his slave, Achilles refuses. He was going to sail home, and he told the other Greeks to follow his example. Patroclus found this reaction to be in poor taste. He could not stand the thought of his fellow Greeks being slaughtered while the Myrmidons stood down.

The Trojans had advanced their attack by this time, as they wished to drive the rest of the Greek army into the sea. Little did they know that Zeus had already prophesied that the Greek army would be the victor in the war, but the king of the gods was not above humbling or punishing the hero that had stepped out of line on the battlefield.

Patroclus went to Achilles and begged him to allow him to fight in the battle. In addition to this request, he also asked permission for the honor of wearing Achilles's armor into battle. Achilles could not deny his most beloved friend's request, but he told Patroclus to only fight long enough to drive the Trojans back from the ships.

Patroclus, filled with courage, ran into the battle, fully outfitted in Achilles's distinct armor. He managed to rally the Greek forces and pushed back the Trojans. He even ended the life of one of Zeus's favorite mortal sons, Sarpedon. Hector had to pull his men back to the safety of the city.

However, Patroclus was driven drunk with blood lust. He knew a potential victory was on the horizon. Some variations say that Apollo robbed him of his senses, which led to Patroclus following the Trojans all the way to the city gates. This was exactly what Achilles had told him not to do. As Patroclus advanced, he took as many Trojan lives as he could.

Eventually, he came face to face with Hector and was slaughtered. With one clean jab of his spear, Hector skewered Patroclus. It wasn't until the end of the battle, when the bodies were being removed from the field to be cremated, that news of Patroclus's death reached Achilles. Every soldier of Greece knew who the man was, and one soldier ran to tell Achilles. He couldn't believe it, but when he saw the body, he dropped to his knees and began to wail. Once his wailing had ceased, Achilles felt nothing but rage and anger toward Hector.

Without authorizing his next move with Agamemnon, Achilles immediately mounted a chariot and drove it all the way to the city gates of Troy. The archers were ready to dispose of the warrior, but Hector ordered them to stand down. He was sure that his skills on the battlefield were akin to, if not better than, Achilles. Hector was also a man of honor and would not simply dispose of Achilles when the warrior had come to his gates seeking one-on-one combat. He would have disgraced his family's name and honor if he did not accept the challenge.

The fight that ensued between the two warriors was a dance of death, as the two men were agile and cunning. Hector eventually began to tire, but Achilles's anger fueled his strength. With one thrust of a spear, it was all over. Hector laid there in the dust as Achilles went over and tied his feet together. He fashioned Hector to the back of his chariot and rode all the way back to camp with the crown prince of Troy dragging behind. The sight was too much for King Priam to behold, and he fainted at the sight of his firstborn and heir being disrespected in such a manner. This also greatly angered the gods, as it displayed a severe lack of honor and self-control, especially since Hector had asked for his body to be treated respectfully. Hector had not singled out Patroclus for a kill; in fact, he had thought he was battling Achilles since Patroclus was wearing his armor. What Achilles did to Hector's body was not necessary in the eyes of many, and the warrior would pay for his offense.

A fresco of Achilles dragging Hector's corpse.
(Public Domain,
https://commons.wikimedia.org/wiki/File:Triumph_of_Achilles_in_Corfu_Achill eion.jpg)

Achilles was brought down by Paris, who was fairly gifted with a bow and commanded the archers high up on the walls of Troy. During another campaign to overtake the city, Paris saw Achilles below in the swarm of blood and bodies. He took aim and let loose his arrow, aiming right for Achilles's exposed leg. The legs were one of the only regions of the body to not be covered by any form of armor. The wound, he thought, would give another soldier enough of a fighting chance to kill Achilles. Little did he know that the gods were on his side. At the last moment, Apollo pushed Achilles a little further so that the arrow went right through the tendon in his heel (hence the name for this body part being the Achilles' heel). This was his only weak point, and it caused the remainder of his organs to shut down. The greatest warrior in all of Greece was defeated and lay in the dust for all to see.

After the death of Achilles, the morale of the Greek army was at its lowest point. The Trojan War lasted ten long years, and it seemed as if the fighting would never cease. The city of Troy had built its walls strong and high, and it was nearly impossible for all the armies of Greece to overtake the city without serious casualties. And now they had lost one of their best warriors. The Myrmidons refused to go onto the battlefield for any other master besides Achilles, not even when Agamemnon threatened them with execution. The kings of Greece were desperately trying to persuade Agamemnon to abandon the campaign and sail home. He feared what would happen to his kingdom if he lost this war, though. If the Trojans could beat him so easily, it might give other empires ideas about invading territories he had worked so hard to acquire.

Then salvation came in the form of an idea, an ingenious and deceitful idea from the mind of Odysseus. He was by far the most cunning and intellectually gifted out of all the Greek kings. He knew that the Trojans were very devout subjects of the gods and that they would never refuse a sacrificial offering.

Odysseus told Agamemnon to have his men break down one of the ships. They would use the planks and the nails to construct an offering that King Priam would not be able to refuse. This offering was the Trojan horse. Inside, the horse would be filled with Greek soldiers. Once they were inside the city walls, the men would open the gate for the remainder of the Greek army. Odysseus told Agamemnon to have all the other ships sail around to the far side of the coast and to leave a lookout so that they could confirm the gift had been received.

Depiction of the Trojan horse on a Corinthian pot, circa 560 BCE. Public Domain,
https://commons.wikimedia.org/wiki/File:Trojan_horse_on_corintian_aryballos.JPG

The lookout in the tower of Troy called out that there were no more Greek ships spotted on the coast. An envoy was sent down to the shores and reported back that the Greeks had, in fact, departed but that they left a gift on their way out. They thought perhaps it was an offering to the god Poseidon for a safe journey home. Some sources say it was an offering to Athena and that by taking the horse into the city gates, Troy would be impregnable.

Cassandra, Priam's eldest daughter, cautioned her father to dispose of the offering by burning it right then and there on the beach. Priam was a man devoted to the gods and would not hear of anyone burning an official offering of such stature, especially to one of the more temperamental gods. The good king decided that the horse would be brought into the city and placed inside the temple of Poseidon (or Athena, depending on which version you read). It would serve as a reminder and honor of the victory won against all the armies of Greece.

However, Cassandra had been cursed by the god Apollo to know the future. This sounds pretty nice, except he made it so that no one believed her. And Priam's decision turned out to be a fatal mistake. When night fell, and the whole city lay in their beds fast asleep and oblivious to the impending danger, the Greek soldiers crawled out from the horse and opened the gates to the city. In a matter of hours, the entirety of Troy was engulfed in flames. We will spare the gory details of what happens when a city is overtaken, but you can use your imagination.

Like Achilles, some Greeks would end up paying for their lack of honor. Even though they had won the war, they did so with trickery and deceit, which was far different from beating your enemies on the open battlefield. Many of the Greeks who sailed for home did not survive the journey, or their trip was delayed by trials and hardships. In fact, when some reached home, they found their wives married to others, having believed that after so many years, their husbands were never coming back. One of the fortunate ones to make it home was Odysseus.

However, before he reunited with his queen Penelope, he would spend several years sailing the ancient world, being tested with a few legendary trials of his own. His story would become one of the most famous myths of all time and one of the first to be put down in writing. We are referring to none other than the *Odyssey*.

Chapter Fourteen: The Odyssey and the Return of Heroes

Many years before Odysseus had been called to fight in Troy, he married his wife Penelope, and the two had a son named Telemachus. It was a joyous day when the prince was born. The entire kingdom rejoiced, but none more so than Anticlea, Odysseus's mother. She saw that her son's happiness was now complete, and if her son was happy, the kingdom would be as well. Odysseus was beloved by the entire kingdom, and his son and heir would grow up amongst the people, learning how a king ruled.

However, Odysseus never got to see his son grow, as he was away for ten long years in the campaign for Troy. And for ten years after the war ended, Odysseus strived to return home to the bed of his wife, Penelope. However, the anger the gods felt toward the Greeks was doubly true for Odysseus. The Trojan horse was his brainchild, and after his plan succeeded, he forgot to pay homage to the god Poseidon, lord of all horses and the master of the seas (the very sea on which Odysseus was to set sail). Odysseus's thoughtlessness created his worst enemy. Poseidon was one of the least forgiving of the gods, and as such, he swore that Odysseus would never again see the shores of his beloved Ithaca. Instead, he would suffer on the high seas and be steered into any potential danger.

During the years Odysseus was trying to get home, a brigade of suitors eventually made their way to the palace. They were led by the vilest amongst their company, Antinous. These suitors made a mess of the king's great hall, but neither Penelope nor Telemachus (now a young man) had the authority or the strength to make the suitors leave. They all believed that the true king was dead and that there would be no consequences for their actions. Meanwhile, Odysseus had already set sail from Troy and vowed that despite Poseidon's vow of destruction, he would return home a victor.

For his first interference, Poseidon set a thick fog over the Aegean, separating Odysseus from the rest of the Greek fleet. The ship sailed aimlessly, as the lookout could see nothing but fog. There seemed to be no end to the sea and no land in sight. Just then, land seemed to appear out of nowhere. The men were hopeful that the island was inhabited by mankind, for they could seek shelter, rest, and perhaps find a new and correct course for Ithaca.

The instant that Odysseus set foot on the island, he knew that it was no place of men. All he could make out in the distance was the faint sound of sheep and goats. Herds would not be without their shepherd, but who and what exactly was the shepherd was the real question to be answered. Odysseus sent two of his scouts to see what the island held. The men found no signs of civilization or manmade structures of any kind. The only thing they found on the whole island was a vast cave that seemed to disappear down into the depths of the earth. In this cave was nothing save for a great deal of goat cheese. But who made the cheese, and where was the master of the herds?

While the men were overjoyed to find this cave of plenty, Odysseus was still hesitant, and the knot in his stomach would not go away. The king was famed for his mind and instincts, which could smell danger a mile away. He found it suspect that the cave contained no tools or weapons of any kind. How did these men fend for themselves, shear their sheep, or create the heavy stone door to the cave?

Outside the cave, Odysseus's men were busy collecting firewood to prepare their evening supper, and they found a large footprint, one that was ten times larger than any print made by a human or animal. Why the men didn't think it necessary to report the print to their leader is unknown. They must have thought that the being who left the print was long dead; things like giants were rarities in the world of the Greeks now. And what were the chances they had stumbled across one? So, Odysseus's men made camp inside the cave and proceeded to get roaringly drunk. The ship had run out of fresh water a while ago, and the Greeks would mix their wine with water; otherwise, it was too strong. The inebriated men continued to laugh and joke, making an excessive amount of noise. This was not the brightest thing to do, considering these men had no idea where they were or whose company they were going to find.

Just then, they felt the earth shake. They could hear the bleating of the sheep not too far off, as well as the deep breath of something very large making its way back to the cave. It was not a shepherd after all but a cyclops by the name of Polyphemus, a son of Poseidon. Polyphemus was astounded to find Odysseus and his men in the cave. He quickly shut the large stone door to his cave and inquired who were these men to be so bold as to eat his food.

Odysseus, ever the politician, decided to try and reason with the cyclops, explaining that they had eaten from his stores but only because they were so hungry. In fact, they wanted to trade goods for the things they had eaten. Polyphemus was not interested in what the men had brought to trade, declaring that he did not eat the food of men but only meat. He then seized one of Odysseus's soldiers, tore the man in two, and ate the upper half of his body. The remaining soldiers leaped to their feet, ready to defend their lives, but Odysseus knew how dangerous it would be to try and fight a cyclops. He told his men to stay calm.

The king was very clever; he told the cyclops that he would be his next meal, willingly and freely. However, if the cyclops ate him, he would never possess the magic inside of Odysseus. It was not uncommon for the world of men and magic to collide, and quite a few mortals had magical gifts similar to that of Phineas the seer or Medea the sorceress. This caught Polyphemus's attention, and he asked for Odysseus's name. Odysseus told him that his name was Nobody (yes, literally nobody) and then offered him some wine to drink. Polyphemus had never heard of or tasted wine, and the cunning king of Ithaca told him that it was the drink of the gods. Cyclopes were looked down upon by most of the immortals; they occupied a lesser status, despite their immense skill and strength. Polyphemus quickly drank the "wine of the gods" while one of Odysseus's soldiers played him a soft lullaby. Polyphemus then fell into a deep sleep. However, the men still had a fairly large issue on their hands. The stone door was immovable. Only the giant cyclops could move the stone and set the men free. However, clever Odysseus had a plan.

He had his soldiers collect all of the sheepskins that Polyphemus used for his bed. He then set about to fashion a giant lance. This he used to blind the cyclops's eye, who ran to the stone door, opened it, and called out to his brothers that Nobody had blinded him. It was a very clever move indeed. The soldiers were then able to sneak past the blinded Polyphemus by wearing the skins of his sheep. Odysseus suffered the loss of a few of his men against the cyclops, but all in all, the company had a fairly impressive survival rate, despite the horrific manner of death their comrades faced.

Laconian pottery showing the blinding of Polyphemus,
circa 565–560 BCE.
Public Domain,
https://commons.wikimedia.org/wiki/File:Odysseus_Polyphemos_Cdm_Paris_190.jpg

The rest of the company returned to the ship and sailed away as fast as they could. From the deck of his ship, Odysseus called out to Polyphemus that his fate to be blinded had been sealed by his own father, Poseidon. If the god had not made the ship veer off course and land on Polyphemus's island, the cyclops would still have his sight. While Odysseus was one of the cleverest kings in the history of Greek mythology, he was known for his immense pride and somewhat boastful nature. The man who thinks he is the smartest in the room is oftentimes the hardest to get along with. These men rarely learn from their mistakes as well. So, it is no surprise that Odysseus was quick to add insult to injury by provoking Poseidon yet again.

The men sailed for months, and their extreme thirst nearly killed them all until they finally saw land. It was yet another strange island with more potential surprises. Odysseus went off on his own to look for water for his men. When he finally found a freshwater source, the stream somehow evaded his pitcher. Every time he lowered the vessel to obtain some of the water, it moved out of his way. Odysseus was sure this was some sort of madness or illusion brought on by extreme thirst or hunger, but it was none other than Poseidon who was refusing the hero and his men the right to a drink of water.

Odysseus then heard the voice of someone. It was the king of the island greeting Odysseus. "I am Aeolus, the keeper of the winds, and this is my island." Aeolus told Odysseus that he meant him and his men no harm and that he actually wanted to help the hero in his quest to return home. Aeolus thought Poseidon was being unfair. In some versions, he actually despises Poseidon, thinking him arrogant and selfish since Poseidon never gave the wind its due credit for its influence over the high seas.

Odysseus and his men got along with Aeolus, and Aeolus was very fond of Odysseus for his clever mind and inquisitive nature. Despite his hubris, Odysseus knew that there was something to be learned from his failures. Aeolus gifted a bag of the winds (minus the east wind) to Odysseus, telling him to use it in his most dire time of need to push his ship all the way home. Soon after, Odysseus and his men returned to the ship and set sail. All Odysseus could think of was returning to his beloved wife, and for the first time in months, he was absolutely sure that he would return to her and their son soon.

However, Odysseus's men were all too curious about what their master had retrieved from the island. What kind of treasure was Odysseus hiding? Most believed it to be gold, and after such a treacherous journey, they expected their fair share. Just then, the lookout called from the top of the crow's nest. The shores of Ithaca were in sight! But the men would not allow the ship to dock until they had opened the sack and retrieved a portion of the gold. They could never have known that the winds were stored inside.

They released the winds, which caused a great storm. The ship was pushed far from Ithaca to the other side of the world. The ship's supplies had gone overboard as well. Just when home was within grasp, it was all taken away. The men despaired, while Odysseus lost his trust and confidence in his crew.

However, there was no time for harsh grudges when survival was on the line. Odysseus sent his men off to find whatever game there was on the island. Then out of nowhere, a pig ran down onto the beach where the remainder of the men were resting. They immediately set about trying to catch and kill the pig to cook it for their evening meal. One of Odysseus's soldiers who was sent on the hunt burst through the bushes; he seemed to have been chasing after the pig as well. He ran toward Odysseus and begged him to stop the men from killing the pig, for it was Polites, one of Odysseus's own soldiers.

All the men laughed in his face until he told them the cause of Polites's affliction. It was a witch, Circe, a great and powerful sorceress. They had landed on her island, and she had turned every last man in the hunting party into animals, all except the one soldier who escaped. Odysseus believed the soldier's tale. He told his men to stay with the ship. If he did not return by sundown, they were to sail away from the island and never look back. Odysseus went ahead alone. He would not risk putting any more of his men in danger.

Just as the soldier had said, Odysseus followed the same path up into the hills, but he came across a giant black bear. In order to avoid the beast, he began to climb the side of the mountain. When he was about to reach the top, Hermes appeared to Odysseus. He had been sent by Athena; she had been watching over the hero since he left his home nearly fifteen years ago. She, too, despised Poseidon and wished for the king of Ithaca to succeed in his quest.

Hermes offered Odysseus an herb from the face of the cliff. He told him to eat this plant for it would protect him from the witch's curse. Hermes told Odysseus that when the witch saw her curse did not affect the king, she would try to conquer him another way—in the bedroom.

Odysseus came across the giant stone palace, which was surrounded by animals of all types: lions, tigers, bears, and a few monkeys—the whole cast of the Wizard of Oz. Then he saw the witch standing in the doorway surrounded by all her animals; he recognized a few of his men amongst the droves of creatures. Each one seemed to be crying out for help. She offered Odysseus wine with honey, a drink the king knew was meant to transform him into an animal. Circe sat back on her throne and waited for her potion to work. Odysseus drank and drank, but he remained a man.

This confused, angered, and aroused the witch. Odysseus pulled out his sword, meaning to end her life, but Circe conveniently reminded him of the fact that his men would remain animals without her magic to change them back. She then made him an offer. She would release Odysseus's men from their captive forms if he took her to bed. As he was having sex with Circe, one by one, his men regained their human forms. She told Odysseus to bring the rest of his men to her palace, and they would eat and drink their fill until they were rested and ready to continue their journey.

Circe Offering the Cup to Ulysses *by John William Waterhouse,*
1891.
Public Domain,
https://commons.wikimedia.org/wiki/File:Circe_Offering_the_Cup_to_Odysseus.jpg

All the while Odysseus was lying in Circe's bed, he still dreamed of his wife, of meeting her again, feeling her embrace, and basking in her smile. Circe noticed this of her hero and inquired how he could lay in her bed every night but still think of his wife? Fair question. Odysseus was by no means a hostage of Circe. He could have left with his men after a few days of rest, but he still found himself returning to her bed of his own volition. Odysseus's men had even asked when they would be leaving, but the great hero had no response. He was happy for the first time in years, and it was hard for him to leave that all behind. He had children with Circe, and they deeply loved each other. He wanted to linger in Circe's bed, whisper sweet nothings to each other, and enjoy each other intimately. Heroes in Greek mythology are sometimes defined more by their faults than by their deeds, and one of Odysseus's biggest faults was his affinity for beautiful goddesses.

Eventually, Odysseus's men were able to convince him that it was time to continue the journey. Circe offered Odysseus advice for finding his way home to Ithaca. She said one man and one man alone would be able to point Odysseus in the right direction. This was Tiresias, the prophet, who had long been dead and was currently living in the underworld. Circe told her lover that he must cross the River Styx and sacrifice a lamb, then enter the flames in order to find the prophet.

The entire time Odysseus sailed for the underworld, he thought of his son, who had now been many years without a father, and his wife, who surely suffered more than anyone. Meanwhile, Penelope's suitors had grown bolder and continued to linger in the king's palace, demanding an answer from her in regard to who was to be her new husband. It was customary that guests could not be turned away, and the men were abusing this custom to the extreme. However, Penelope was just as clever as her husband and managed to avoid their pestering questions by keeping them in either a state of drunkenness or sleep. She told them that she would choose a suitor once she had completed a shroud for her husband. It was incredibly large, and she unraveled the shroud little by little at the end of the day in order to buy more time. Her suitors remained so inebriated that they didn't even notice.

In the meantime, Odysseus and his company had reached the entrance to the land of the dead. There lay a river of fire ahead that Odysseus had to cross, and he had to cross it alone. Odysseus bid his men a tearful goodbye, as they were sure their master would perish in the flames. Odysseus took his lamb and went forth in search of Tiresias. He found the blind prophet in the depths of the underworld, sitting at the edge of the river of fire, his feet dangling into the waters like he was on vacation in hell. Odysseus made his request and tossed the lamb into the flaming waters. Tiresias then told him that in order to find his way home, he needed to use the constellation Orion and sail toward its brightest star until he reached the straits of Scylla, an insatiable monster of the deep. On one side of the strait would be Scylla, while on the other would be Charybdis, the swirling maelstrom of death.

Before Odysseus returned to his men, his mother Anticlea appeared before him. Odysseus felt a great wave of grief pass over him, for he knew his mother had perished while he had been away. Little did he know she took her own life in her grief, as she had been waiting for a son that never returned. Anticlea told her son to make haste and return to Ithaca as soon as possible, for the nobles of his kingdom sought to make his wife their own, and Penelope was running out of strength and reasons to resist marrying one of the suitors. It was customary, after all, for a queen to remarry if her husband had been declared dead. Good thing for her that Odysseus's death was still speculation, but that could not last forever. The thing that weighed most heavily on the queen's heart was her son's despair that his father had either perished at Troy or on the seas. Of course, there was the lingering doubt that he had decided simply not to return to his wife and child.

Before Odysseus and his men approached the straits of Scylla, they would have to make their way past the Sirens. The Sirens chanted a beautiful song that caused mortals to drive their ships onto the rocks. It is hotly debated whether the Sirens feasted on the sailors or simply trapped them there, causing sailors to starve since they were unable to leave the beauty of the Sirens' song. Odysseus had received a warning from Circe about the Sirens before he departed her island. She told the king not to listen to the words of the Sirens and that he and his men should plug their ears with beeswax.

Odysseus was an incredibly curious man; he liked to know things that other men did not. One of the things he desired to know was the song of the Sirens. He ordered his men to tie him to the mast of the ship and plug their ears with beeswax. No matter how much he pleaded and cried, they were not to let him loose from his restraints. If he managed to wriggle free, they could not under any circumstances let him enter the water. His men did as they were told, and no matter how their king pleaded and struggled, the men kept sailing as Odysseus listened to the enchanting song of the Sirens.

Odysseus and his men eventually approached the straits of Scylla. Although Odysseus and his men had braved the horrors of the ancient world, they could never have imagined what awaited them in the dark corridor that lay ahead. As they slowly inched their way into the straits, all the light disappeared. It was blacker than any darkness of the night. The air was thick and hot, but the worst part of the whole experience was the quiet. There was absolutely nothing to be heard; even the waves ceased to make noise against the ship. Then, from the darkness, a giant set of jaws lunged forward and snatched one of Odysseus's men from the deck.

It was a horrific sight. The teeth of Scylla were razor-sharp, and the force of her jaws cut the soldier clean in two. His upper body seemingly disappeared into her jaws, and his legs remained upright on the deck of the ship. The men were horrified as the poor soldier's legs began to twitch, his nerve endings unaware that they had been severed from the brain. Scylla then emerged from her dark hiding place. Her form was a grotesque machine of murder, with six long necks, each topped by a single head with razor-sharp teeth. Her claws kept her mounted among the caverns of the narrow corridor. Petrified, Odysseus's men pulled forward. They knew they were unable to best this beast through strength; their only hope was to keep rowing forward and to stay as far from the sides of the cavern as possible.

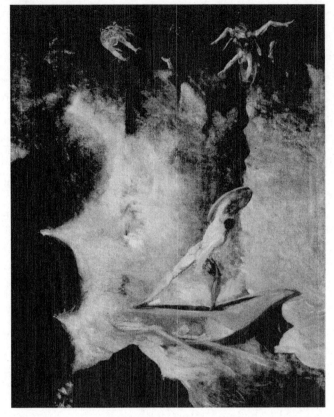

Odysseus in front of Scylla and Charybdis *by Henry Fuseli, 1794–1796.*
Public Domain,
https://commons.wikimedia.org/wiki/File:Johann_Heinrich_F%C3%BCssli_054.jpg

They could see the light at the end of the tunnel and rowed furiously toward what they believed to be their salvation, but it was not what they suspected. Soon enough, Odysseus realized that at the end of the strait was a drop, one that led right into the jaws of Charybdis, a creature even more terrifying than Scylla. Her jaws were not filled with teeth but rather rushing water; she was a massive whirlpool. And the ship was headed straight for the drop, and there was nothing that any of the men could do to stop it. Odysseus told his men to jump and try to catch the vines that hung from the ceiling of the opening. Some of the men made the jump, but most did not, falling into the terrifying maelstrom. Odysseus instructed the remainder of his men to let go of the vines, and they all fell into the sea. When Odysseus surfaced, he called out for his men, but none answered. He was utterly alone, floating in an endless sea. Perhaps Odysseus had finally been bested by Poseidon.

Just then, from out of nowhere, appeared an island of white limestone. Odysseus used the last of his strength to swim toward the island and pulled his body onto the soft sand. He had never been happier to see land. From the tall cliffs, he could make out several figures and heard the soft melody of women's voices in the wind. This was Ogygia, the island of the nymph Calypso, a daughter of the Titan Atlas. It was only her and her maidens who occupied the island, and Odysseus was the first man they had seen in a long time. The beauty of the goddess was legendary; she could be compared to the legendary Helen of Troy or even the goddess Aphrodite herself.

Calypso brought Odysseus water and food until he fell into a deep sleep. Odysseus stirred and tossed with nightmares of his journey, the evil things he had seen, the blood he had seen shed, and the terrible loss of his men who had braved the perils of the world for their king. They were all now dead. Calypso came to his side to rouse him. When he woke, he began to weep uncontrollably and fell into her arms. It did not take very long for the goddess's charms and magic to seep their way into Odysseus's blood, making his heart race. The two fell into one another's embrace, and for the second time on his journey, Odysseus was unfaithful to his wife. Only this time, there was no ulterior incentive to save the lives of his men. This mistake was born from the deepest sadness and loneliness a man could feel.

The two became intense lovers, and he confided in Calypso about the terror of the last thirteen years. He requested a ship from

Calypso so that he might return to Ithaca. However, the goddess informed her newest love that there was none to be had on the island. No one came to her island, and no one was permitted to leave. Odysseus tried to escape once or twice by trying to flag down ships he saw on the horizon, but they were all too far away, and the island was nearly invisible to all, the white limestone hiding it in the glare of the sun. Calypso told Odysseus that he would never leave, as she would never let him go.

Meanwhile, in Ithaca, Telemachus was preparing a ship to set sail in search of Odysseus. He was going to leave without one word to his mother. While he was still pondering the implications of his decision to leave, the gray-eyed Athena appeared to the prince on the beach. She told him to sail to Pylos and Sparta to the court of Menelaus for reasons unknown to Telemachus.

For seven years, Calypso kept Odysseus on her island, his memories of Penelope fading more and more with each passing day. He was wrapped in the arms of the goddess every night. (Some say it wasn't consensual on the part of Odysseus, though. In that version, he was more than ready to sail home.) Odysseus felt that the gods had all but abandoned him to be the hostage of a very deranged and clingy woman. However, Athena had not turned his back on the hero. Over time, she made the king of the gods take notice of Odysseus, of his strength, wit, and cunning mind. These two gods would not see Odysseus end his days as a captive. So, Zeus sent Hermes to Calypso, demanding that she release the hero. Calypso cursed the gods, accusing them of being jealous that she was finally happy with a companion. Hermes advised her not to deny Zeus's command.

According to some accounts, Calypso had been blessed with two children by Odysseus. She was happy keeping Odysseus under her enchantment and raising her children. But what could a nymph do against the will of the gods? She told Odysseus he had to go, that he had to leave her island and her sight. There was driftwood on a nearby island, which Odysseus would use to build his ship. Calypso tried everything in her power to make Odysseus stay; she used sweet words, kisses, tears, and even the promise of immortality, but it made no difference. Odysseus thanked the goddess for saving his life and the supplies she gave him and then pushed his driftwood dingy into the sea.

Back in Ithaca, things had begun to take a turn for the worst for Penelope. After seducing one of her maids, Antinous learned why Penelope's shroud was not yet completed after weeks of work. (Some sources say that he even slept with Penelope, while others say that a slave found out and disclosed the information.) He confronted Penelope and gave the shroud to the other suitors to destroy, desecrate, and burn. Penelope was now alone. She had been outed, she was without hope, and her son was far away in Sparta. Telemachus had made the journey to the house of Menelaus and propositioned the king to aid him in the search for Odysseus. Menelaus informed the prince that his father was still alive. He gained this knowledge from Proteus, the prophet and sea god. The king told Telemachus to remain strong; Odysseus would do whatever it took to return to Ithaca.

On the high seas, Poseidon sought another chance to take his revenge against Odysseus for blinding his son Polyphemus. He battered Odysseus with wind, waves, and rain. Odysseus likely thought that surely this would be the end of his days. How would he survive wandering the high seas if his ship was destroyed? Eventually, Odysseus washed up onto the shores of Scheria, which was home to the Phaeacians. He was found in a weakened state by Princess Nausicaa and carried to the palace of the king. There, he received a warm welcome from the king and queen, who were only too aware of who Odysseus was and what his name meant amongst the warriors of Greece. They begged Odysseus to share his tale and how he had come to survive the wrath of the gods. In return, the king would provide Odysseus a ship and the finest mariners in all his land to man it.

Odysseus recounted all of his treacherous misfortunes to the king and his entire court from the time he left Troy until his departure from Ogygia. No one had ever heard such a story of bravery and terror. The king kept his word, and in the morning, Odysseus set sail, finally for his home country. Every night he slept aboard the ship, he dreamed of Penelope. He could not wait to share their bed together once more and finally meet his son, who had been born just before he left for the Trojan War.

When Odysseus arrived on the shores of Ithaca, he wept from joy. He knew the scent of sweet sea air mixed with pine, and he embraced the feel of the sun cascading from between the branches of the forest as he made his way up to the hut of his faithful swine herder, Eumaeus. When the two men locked eyes, Eumaeus dropped to his knees, buried his face in his hands, and joined Odysseus in weeping. From the port below, Eumaeus could make out the ship of Telemachus returning home from Sparta. Eumaeus rushed to the docks, pulled the prince aside, and told him to follow him back up to his hut; he would not tell the prince why, but when they approached, Odysseus revealed himself. Telemachus was suspicious of this man, but having prior knowledge of his father's whereabouts and the word of Eumaeus to boot, he quickly came to believe that this was his father, Odysseus. The last twenty years of Odysseus's suffering seemed to melt away the moment he embraced his son for the second time in his life. Father and son then sat down to concoct a plan to massacre the suitors and restore Odysseus to his throne. He told Telemachus to join the suitors at their usual feast of barbary later that night and to tell no one that Odysseus had returned to Ithaca.

Up at the palace, Penelope had developed a plan all her own to rid herself of the suitors once and for all. She told them that she would marry the man that was able to string Odysseus's bow and fire it through the eyes of twelve rows of axes (that would be through the end of the hilt where there was typically a metal circle). This was an extraordinary task that had only ever been completed by the king himself.

With the help of Athena, Odysseus was disguised as a beggar (many versions say he was disguised when Telemachus came to see him). He entered the palace and found the contest for Penelope's hand in full swing. He saw the untold mess and filth of the guests that had been plaguing his home for all those years. His rage was great, but he held his tongue, knowing that at any moment, his chance for revenge would come. And at that time, Athena would be with him. That night, Odysseus's nurse from infancy, Eurycleia, came to tend to what she thought was an old beggar. However, from one deep look in his eyes, she knew the man's true identity. It was Odysseus, her Odysseus, the boy she had pulled from the womb of Anticlea herself. She wept tears of joy. Eurycleia wanted to run and tell her mistress Penelope, but Odysseus made her swear not to speak a word of his return, or all hope would be lost.

None of the suitors were able to accomplish the impossible task that Penelope had set for them. None of them could even string the bow. When it seemed as if no one would be able to finish it, the suitors began to grumble. She had to pick someone. A beggar stepped forward and asked to try his hand. The other men scoffed, believing there was absolutely no chance that a man of such lowly stature could wield a bow as fine as this. But they eventually agreed to let him try.

Odysseus walked up and took up the bow. Everyone in the hall watched in amazement as the decrepit old man strung the bow with astonishing ease. He placed one of the arrows on the string and fired it through the hoops of all twelve axes. As he completed the feat, Athena's spell was broken, and Odysseus was revealed. While the contest had been in full swing, Odysseus's loyal servants, Eumaeus and Eurycleia, had been collecting all the suitors' weapons and armor. They then locked the doors of the great hall. And once the contest was over, Odysseus and Telemachus, along with a few of Odysseus's loyal servants, began to massacre the suitors without mercy, one by one.

Odysseus and Telemachus Massacre the Suitors of Penelope *by Thomas Degeorge, 1812.*
Credit: VladoubidoOo, CC BY-SA 3.0 via Wikimedia Commons;
https://commons.wikimedia.org/wiki/File:Thomas_Degeorge_Ulysse.jpg

Later that night, Odysseus was waiting for Penelope in their chambers. Words have not been invented yet for the love these two shared for one another. For twenty years, Odysseus had strived to return to his home, to his wife, to his son, and at long last, that dream was now a reality. He had faced monsters, gods, sexually "enslaving" goddesses, and many other enemies. No mortal man had ever earned such favor from the gods. His mind and iron will were his greatest strengths, but all men need something to live for.

As he and his wife lay in each other's arms for the first time in two decades, he whispered to Penelope that she would never be without him again; she was his world. The story of Odysseus does not end there. It goes on, and today, it inspires people with its many lessons of love, loss, bravery, pride, and friendship. Most of all, the story teaches us that no matter how small we are in the grand scheme of things, we are still able to make all the difference in our own worlds if we are guided equally by our minds and our hearts.

Conclusion

Greek mythology is, for the most part, still entirely relevant in our day and age. Well, no man has ever tried to seduce a woman while in the form of a bird, but we still fall in love, get jealous, act rashly, involve ourselves in good and bad affairs, and strive to find a place of meaning and understanding within the world.

The world began with absolutely nothing, the end of nothing, in fact. And from the darkness emerged a single spark of hope. The Greeks' tales of the cosmic beginning of the world were not so different from the way other ancient cultures viewed the beginning of time, as they have elements of both femininity and masculinity. Gaia was a necessity, just like her husband, Uranus. In fact, Gaia's horrid treatment at the hands of her husband and progeny can be a lesson for the ills mankind inflict on the earth today.

Still, the two halves of femininity and masculinity made one whole perfect world, and it was then subdivided into gods and goddesses, the various representations of what is masculinity and what is femininity. This split dichotomy can be seen in everything that inhabits Greek mythology. The Minotaur was a man, while the monster Scylla was a female. It is no accident that rage, fury, and destruction were embodied by Poseidon, the male god of the seas, just as it was no accident that true wisdom resided in the domain of women, which was embodied by the goddess Athena. Both male and female deities were needed for the ancient Greeks to be able to navigate their world and understand its building blocks, which could be found in everything they could see and touch. Human beings learned how to be human beings from the world surrounding them.

As we have learned by reviewing the myths of heroes, mankind did not always follow the lessons it was provided by the gods and the natural world. Even the best among mortal men and demi-gods made mistakes, and sometimes they learned from it, and other times they didn't. For all his wisdom and wit, Odysseus nearly perished several times due to his prideful nature. Herakles, for all his strength, could not bring his loved ones back from the dead and so had to work through that sadness with the twelve labors, confronting and dealing with his sins while doing so. For all he had achieved, Jason felt the greatest loss of any hero at the end of his days, which just goes to show that success does not bring a person happiness. From Theseus, we can learn to be grateful for the things we have and the help that others are willing to give us, lest karma comes to exact terrible vengeance.

The sheer fact that the gods and goddesses of Greek mythology were subject to and the originators of certain emotions and actions that were also felt and expressed by mankind speaks to the divinity of everyday human life. The final lesson we can glean from Greek mythology is that to be human does not mean to be "other." We are not set apart from everyone and everything else in the world. To be human is to be a part of and subject to a divine world order.

Here's another book by Enthralling History that you might like

Free limited time bonus

Stop for a moment. We have a free bonus set up for you. The problem is this: we forget 90% of everything that we read after 7 days. Crazy fact, right? Here's the solution: we've created a printable, 1-page pdf summary for this book that you're reading now. All you have to do to get your free pdf summary is to go to the following website: **https://livetolearn.lpages.co/enthrallinghistory/**

Once you do, it will be intuitive. Enjoy, and thank you!

Bibliography

https://www.greekmythology.com/Myths/The_Myths/The_Creation/the_creation.html

https://www.theoi.com/articles/what-is-the-greek-creation-myth

https://classicalwisdom.com/mythology/gods/in-the-beginning-part-1

https://www.theoi.com/Titan/TitanKoios.html

Hesiod, *Theogony* 133 & 207 (trans. Evelyn-White) (Greek epic C8th or C7th B.C.)

Beall, E. F. "Hesiod's Prometheus and Development in Myth." Journal of the History of Ideas 52, no. 3 (1991): 355–71.

https://doi.org/10.2307/2710042

https://grbs.library.duke.edu/article/viewFile/6661/5061

https://www.thoughtco.com/the-five-ages-of-man-111776

https://www.britannica.com/topic/Deucalion

https://www.thoughtco.com/people-around-hercules-Herakles-hcrakles-118960

https://www.history.com/topics/ancient-history/hercules

http://www.perseus.tufts.edu/Herakles/amazon.html

https://classicalwisdom.com/mythology/spotlight-on-mythology-theseus-and-theminotaur

https://www.theoi.com/articles/the-myth-of-perseus-and-medusa-explained

https://www.britannica.com/topic/Andromeda-Greek-mythology

https://www.theoi.com/articles/jason-and-the-argonauts-myth

https://www.britannica.com/topic/Jason-Greek-mythology

https://www.theoi.com/Georgikos/KentaurosKheiron.html

https://www.greeka.com/thessaly/pelion/myths/jason-argonauts

http://www.argonauts-book.com/hypsipyle.html

https://www.theoi.com/Pontios/Glaukos.html

https://www.theoi.com/Nymphe/NympheMelia4.html

https://www.theoi.com/Pontios/NereisThetis.html

https://www.theoi.com/Pontios/Nereus.html

https://www.theoi.com/Olympios/JudgementParis.html

https://www.theoi.com/articles/short-trojan-war-summary

https://www.theoi.com/articles/was-achilles-a-warrior

https://www.sparknotes.com/lit/odyssey/summary

https://www.theoi.com/Pontios/Skylla.html

https://www.theoi.com/Nymphe/NympheKalypso.html

Printed in Great Britain
by Amazon

85502073R00098